PINK FLOYD THE ENDLESS RIVER

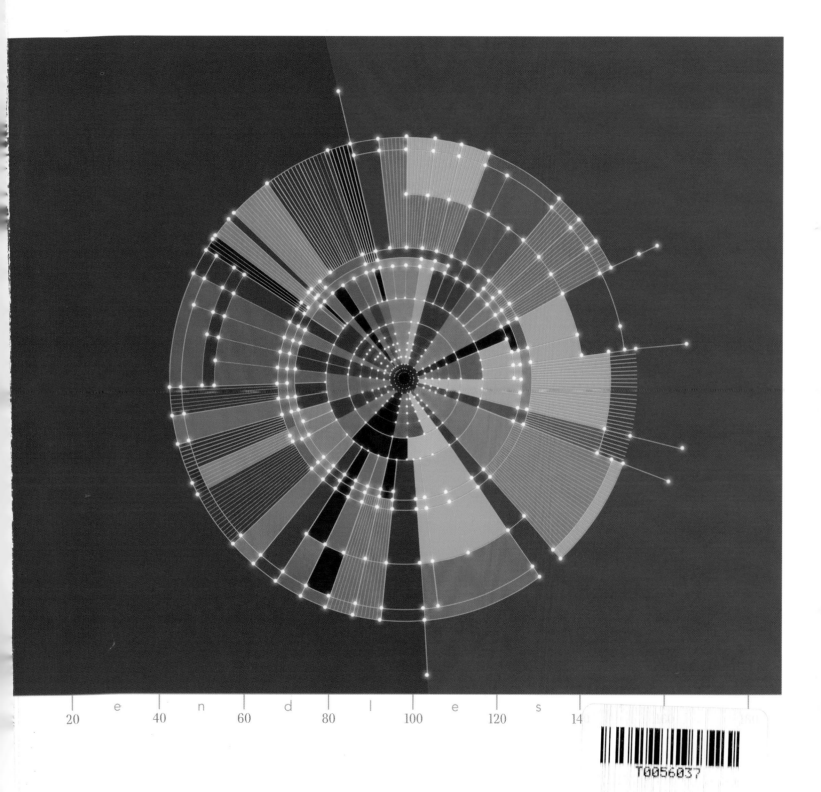

HAL•LEONARD®
CORPORATION

7777 W. BLUEMOUND RD. P.O. BOX 13819 MILWAUKEE, WI 53213

T0056037

t   h   e   e   n   d   l   e
180   160   140   120   100   80   60   40   20

s   s   s   r   i   v   e   r

20   40   60   80   100   120   140   160   180

THINGS LEFT UNSAID ⟿ 9
IT'S WHAT WE DO ⟿ 13
EBB AND FLOW ⟿ 20
SUM ⟿ 22

the end line

180   t   160   h   140   e   120   100   e   80   n   60   d   40   l   20   e

SKINS ⟿ 28
UNSUNG ⟿ 29
ANISINA ⟿ 30
THE LOST ART OF CONVERSATION ⟿ 34
ON NOODLE STREET ⟿ 36

NIGHT LIGHT  40
ALLONS-Y (1) 43
AUTUMN '68 48
ALLONS-Y (2) 50

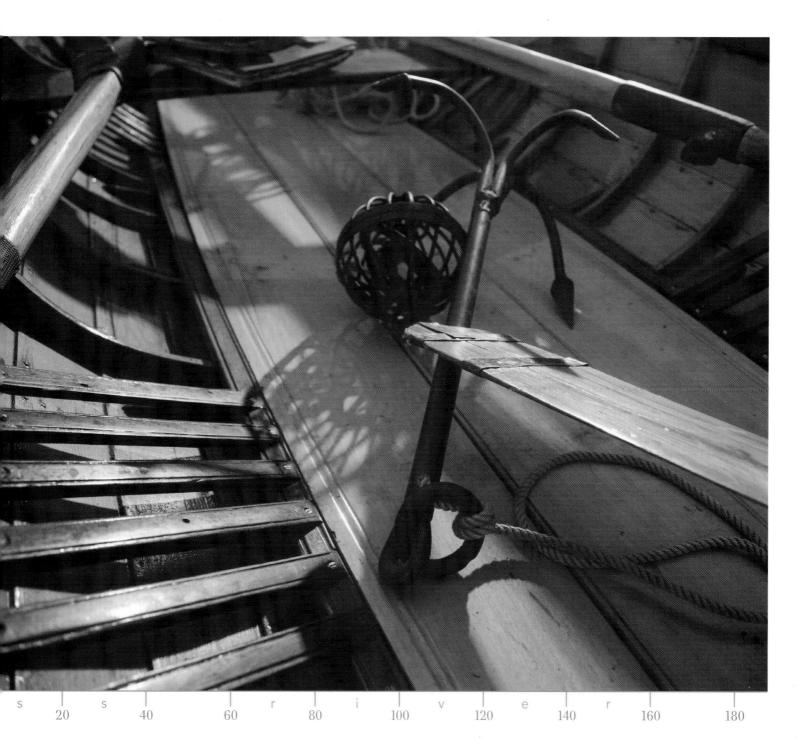

TALKIN' HAWKIN' 54
CALLING 61
EYES TO PEARLS 64
SURFACING 68
LOUDER THAN WORDS 78

r   r   i   v   e   r   r

20   40   60   80   100   120   140   160   180

THINGS LEFT UNSAID

Music by David Gilmour & Richard Wright

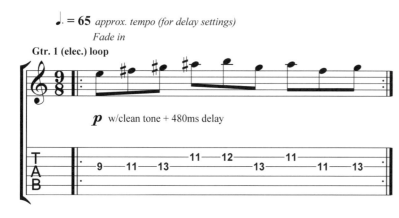

Gtr. 1 (elec.) loop

♩. = **65** *approx. tempo (for delay settings)*
Fade in

p w/clean tone + 480ms delay

Loop cont. w/FX, gradual crescendo + speech samples

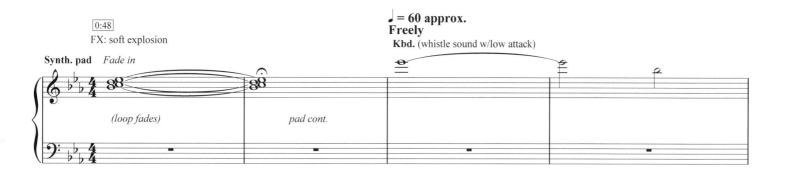

0:48
FX: soft explosion

♩ = **60 approx.**
Freely

Kbd. (whistle sound w/low attack)

Synth. pad *Fade in*

(loop fades)

pad cont.

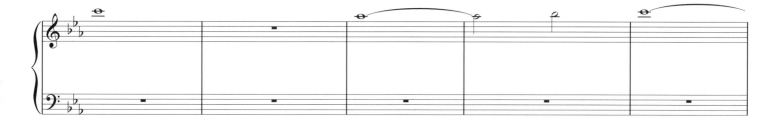

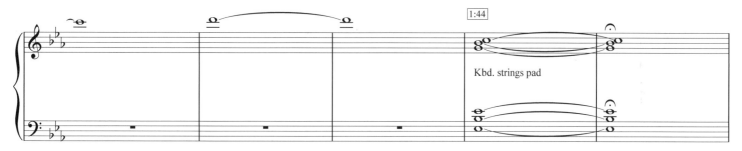

1:44

Kbd. strings pad

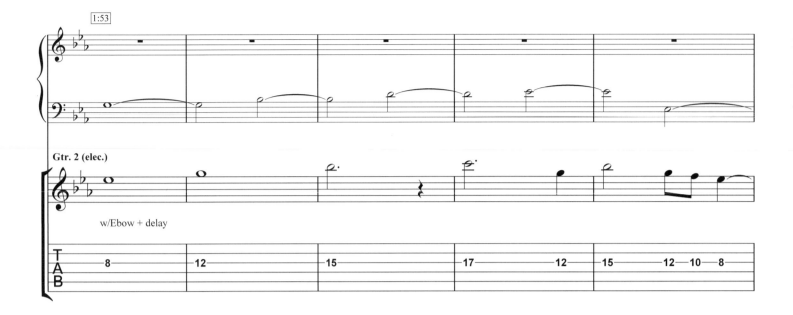

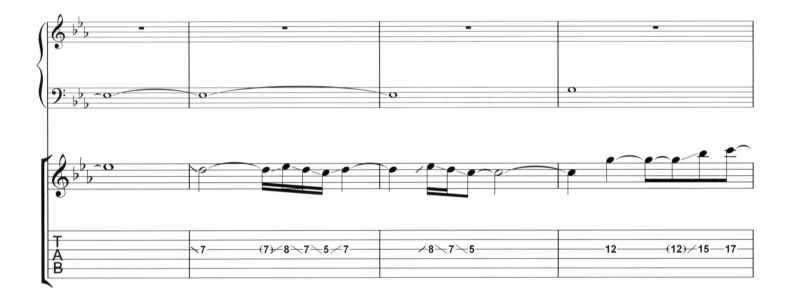

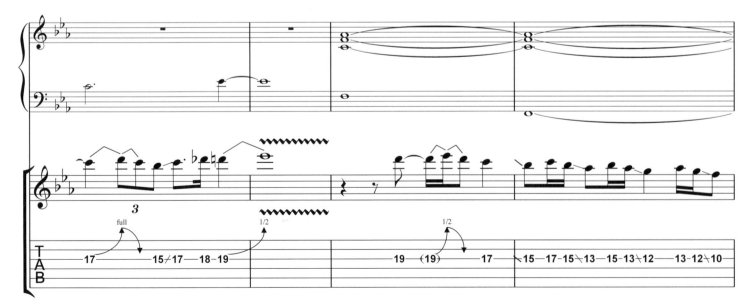

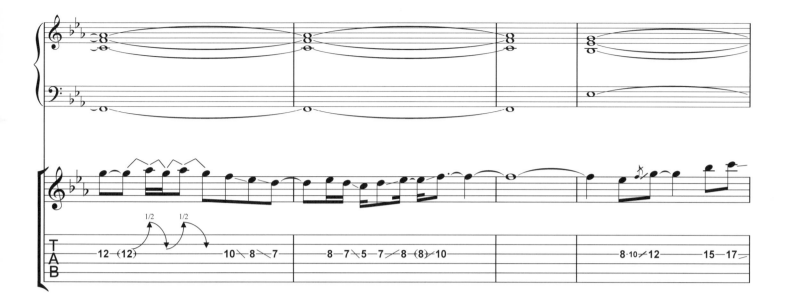

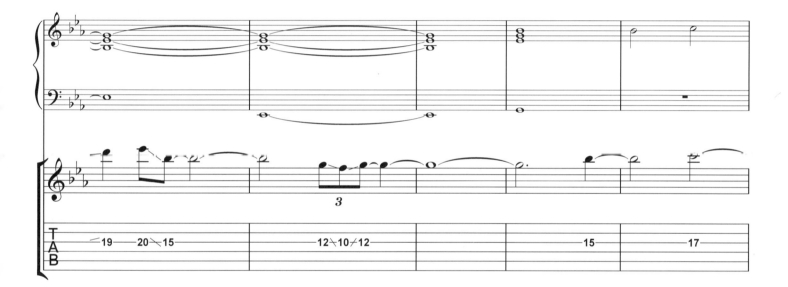

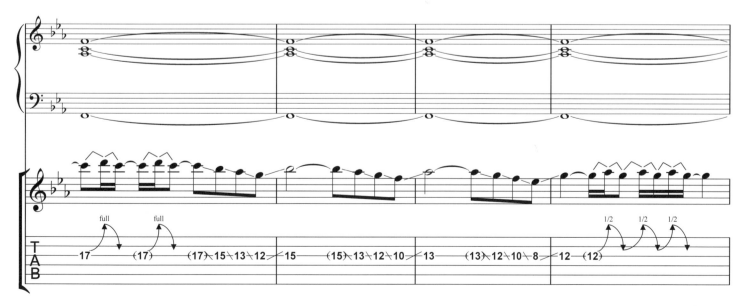

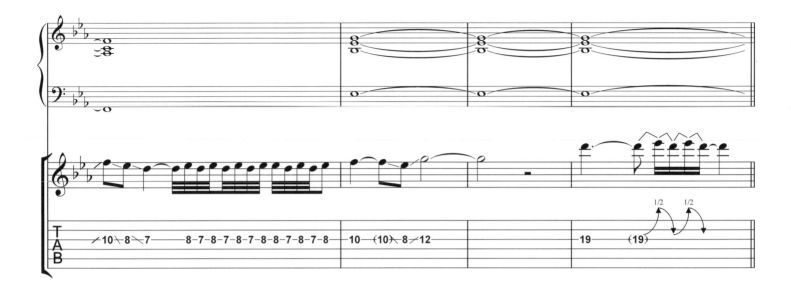

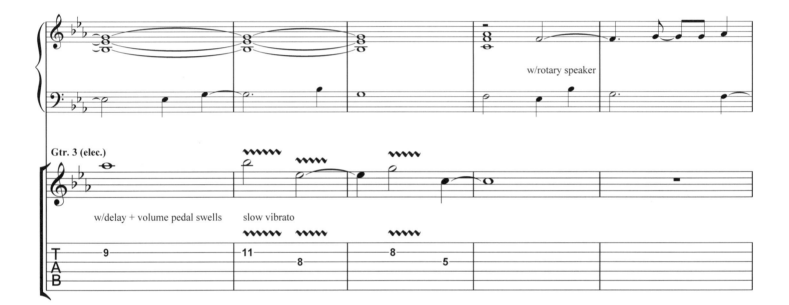

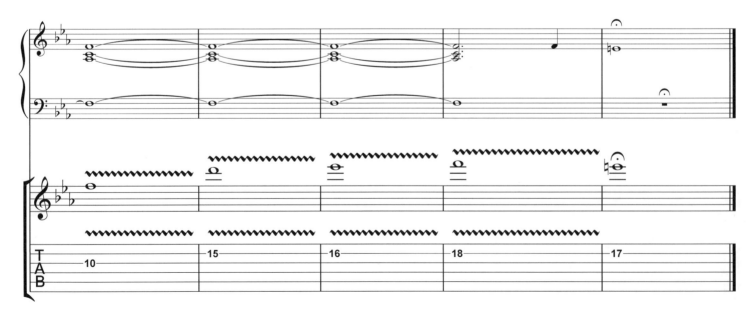

12

IT'S WHAT WE DO

Music by David Gilmour & Richard Wright

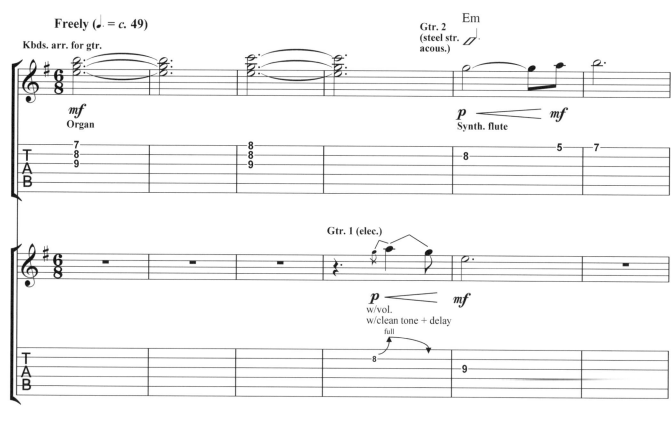

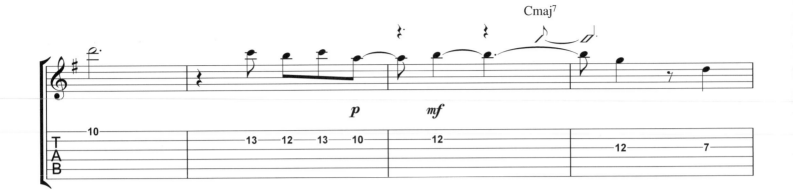

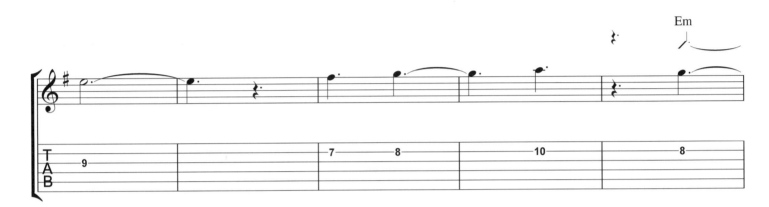

Gtr. solo

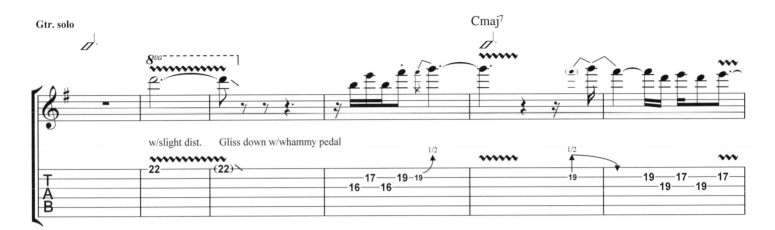

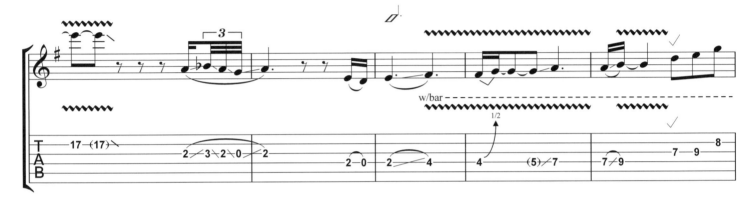

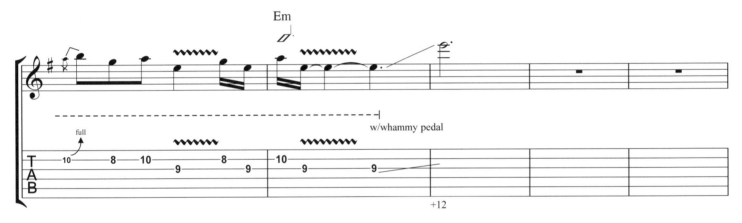

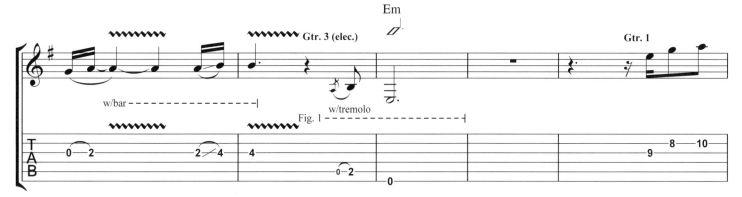

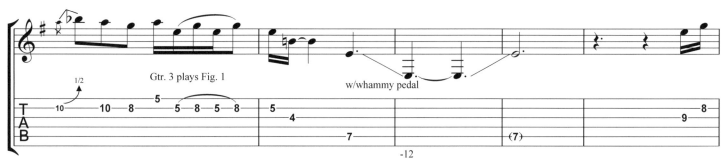

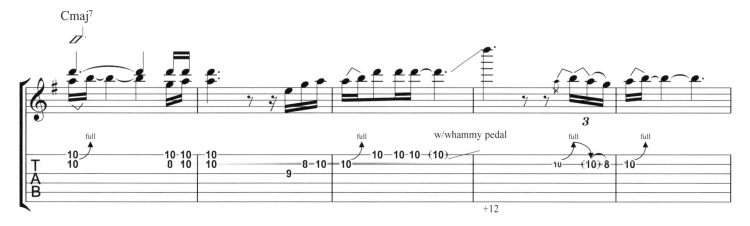

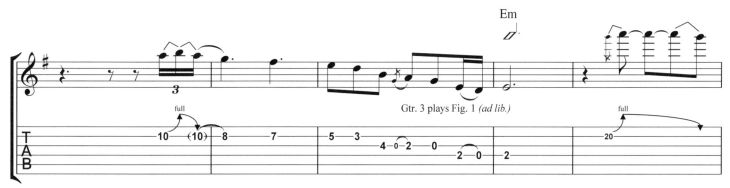

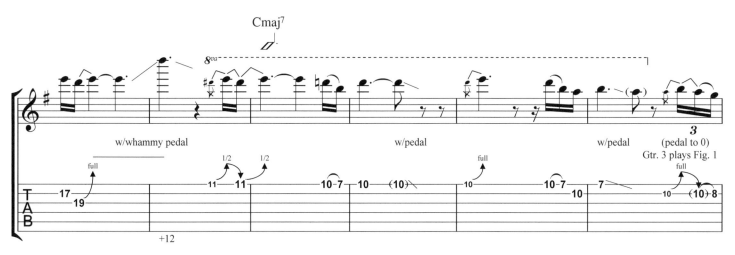

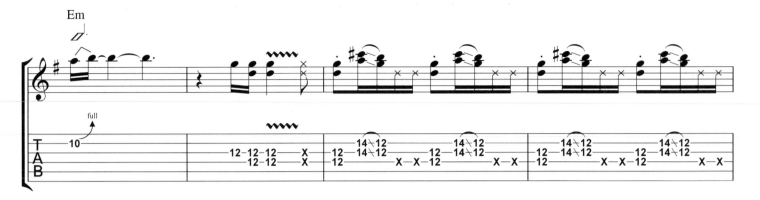

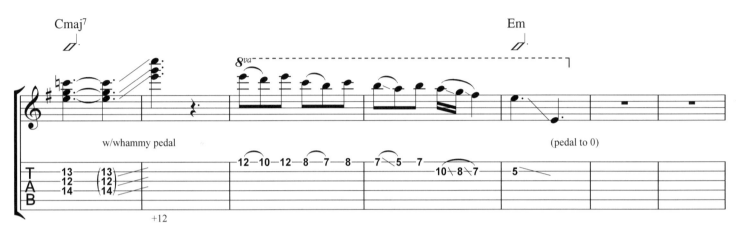

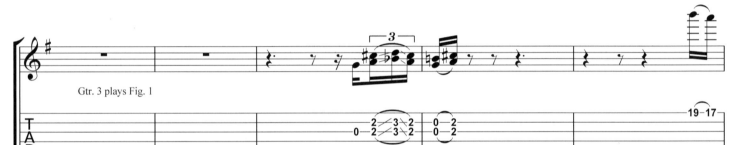

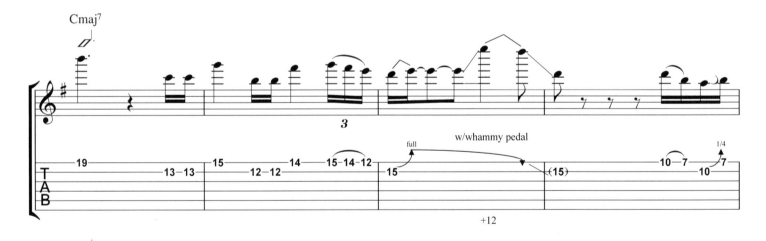

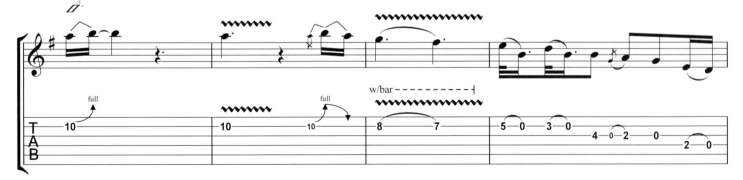

18

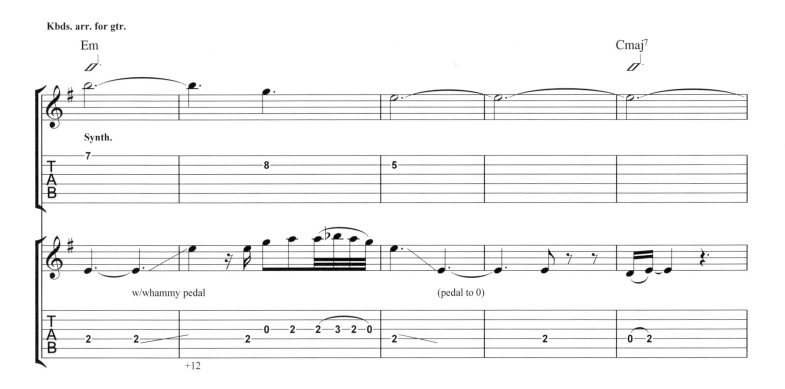

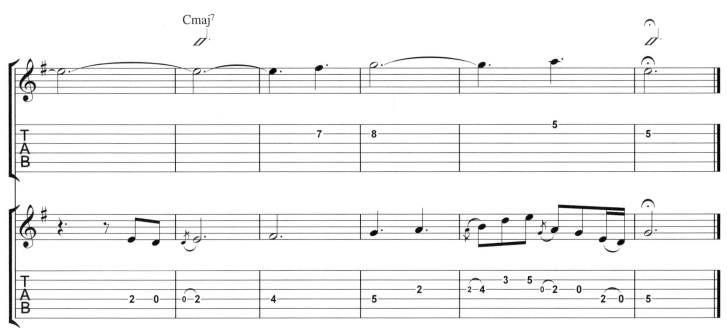

19

EBB AND FLOW

Music by David Gilmour & Richard Wright

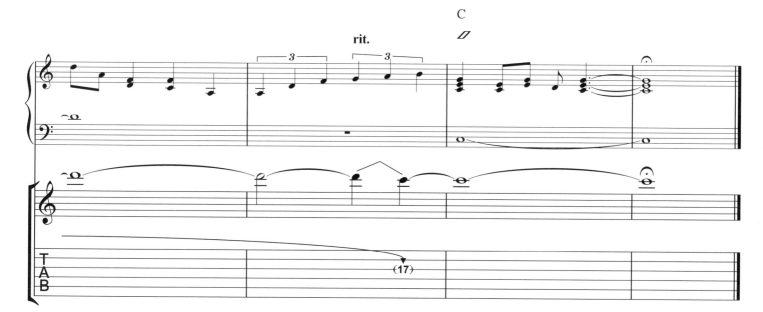

SUM

Music by David Gilmour, Nick Mason & Richard Wright

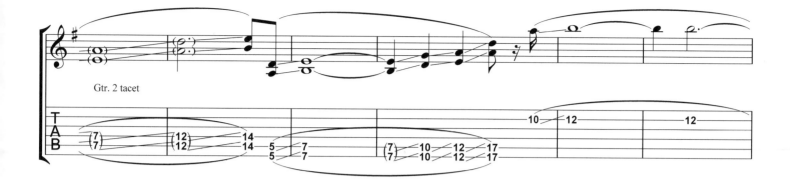

Gtr. 2 tacet

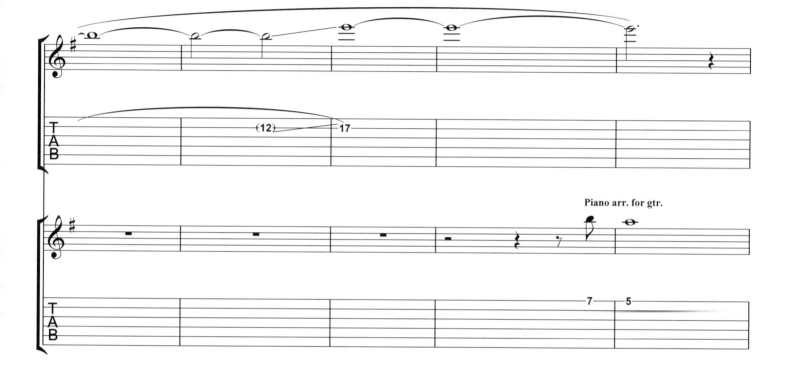

Piano arr. for gtr.

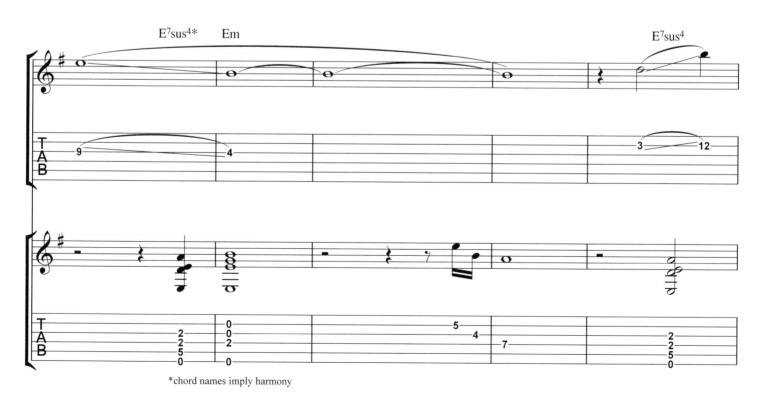

E⁷sus⁴*   Em   E⁷sus⁴

*chord names imply harmony

23

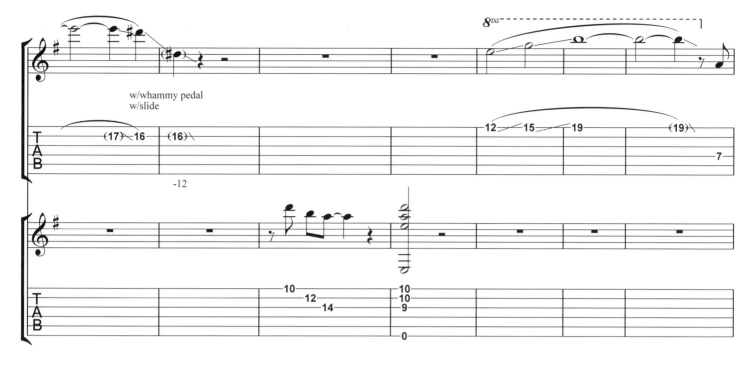

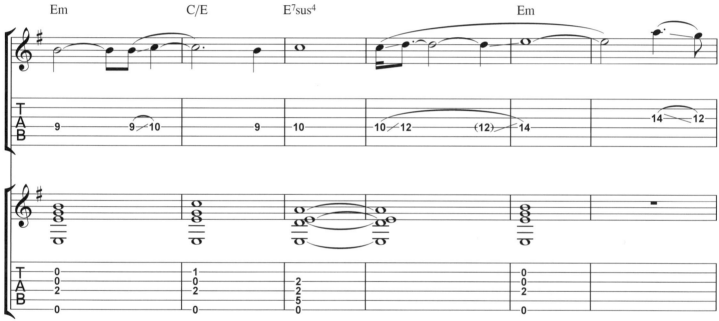

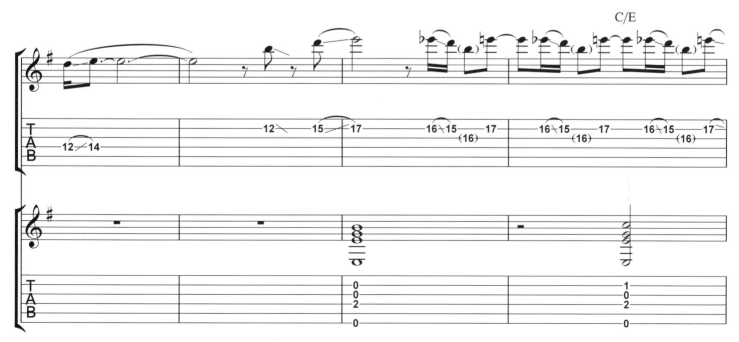

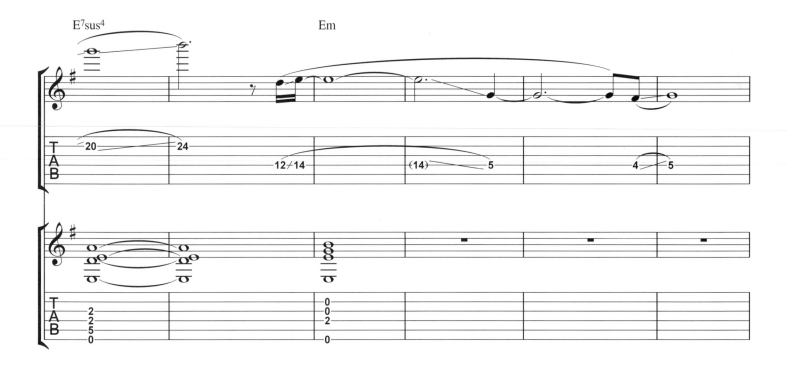

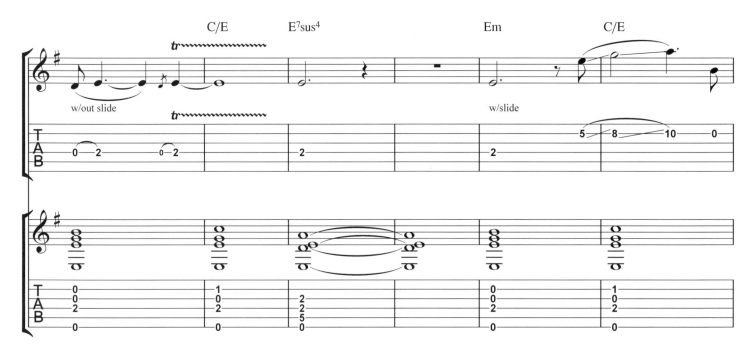

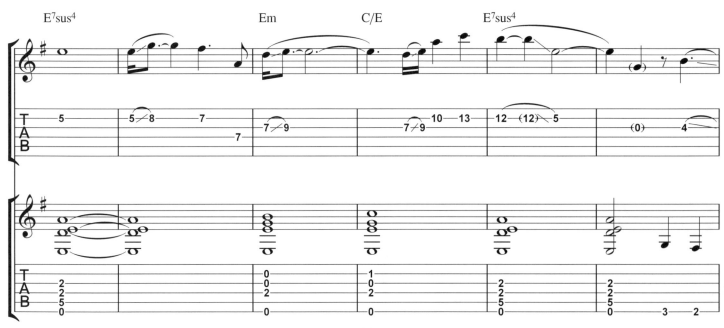

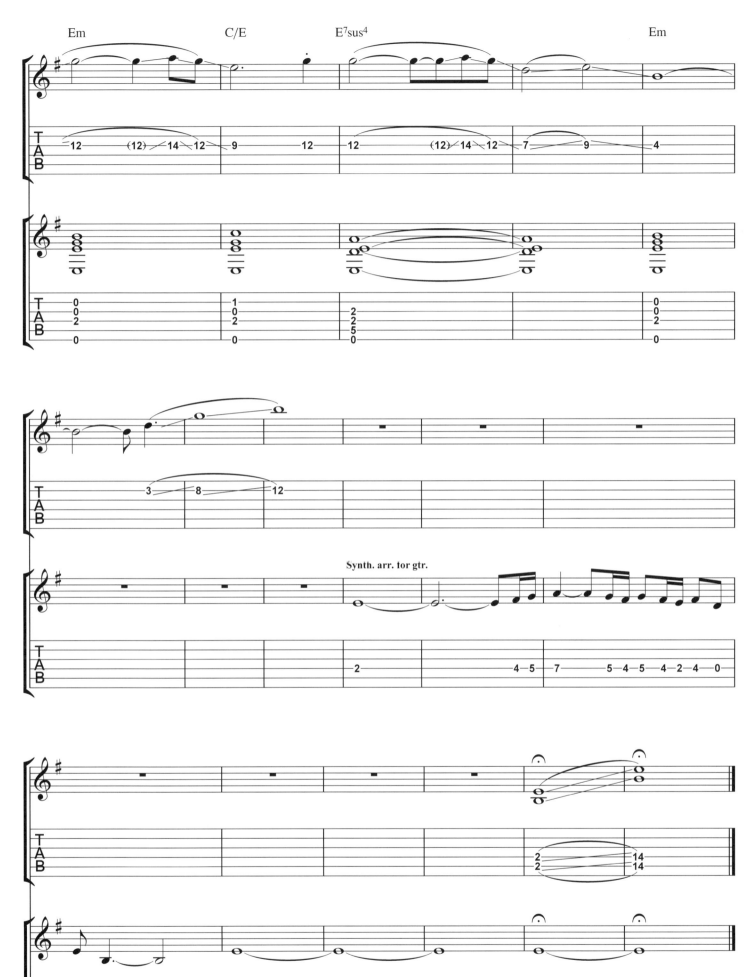

SKINS

Music by David Gilmour, Nick Mason & Richard Wright

UNSUNG

Music by Richard Wright

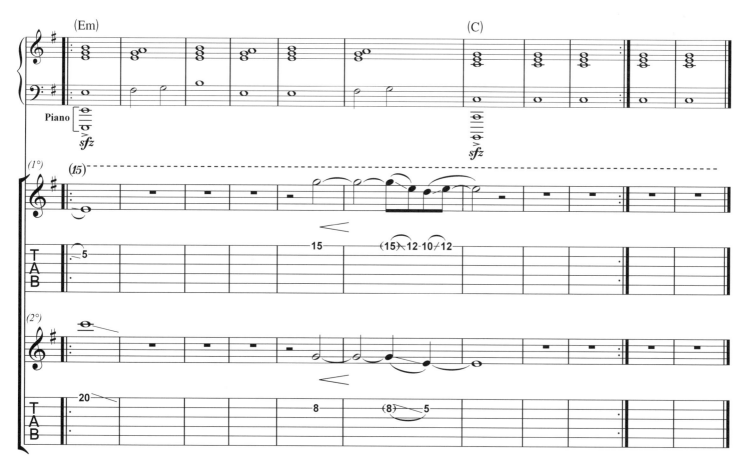

ANISINA

Music by David Gilmour

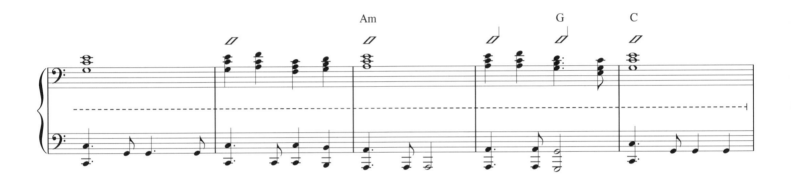

31

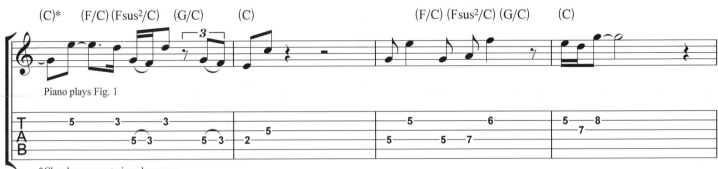

Piano plays Fig. 1

*Chords represent piano harmony

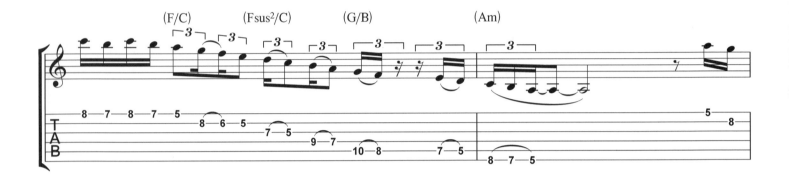

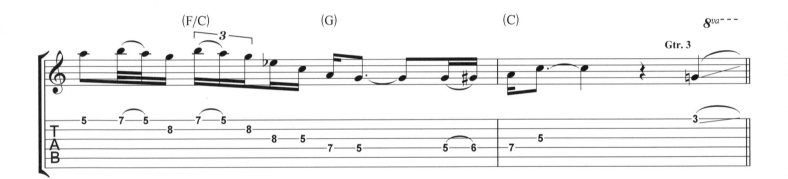

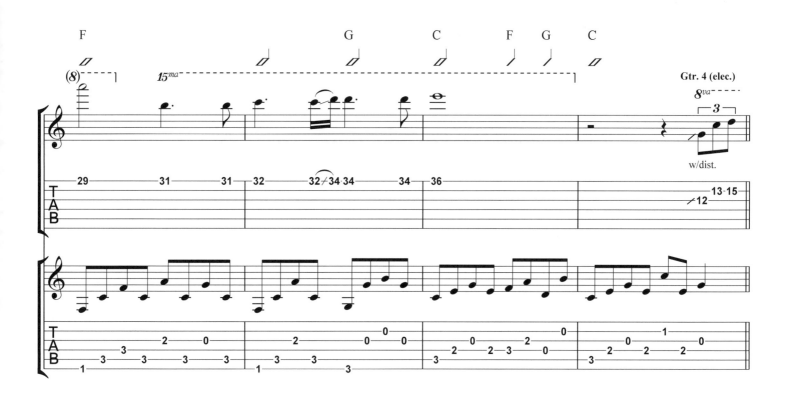

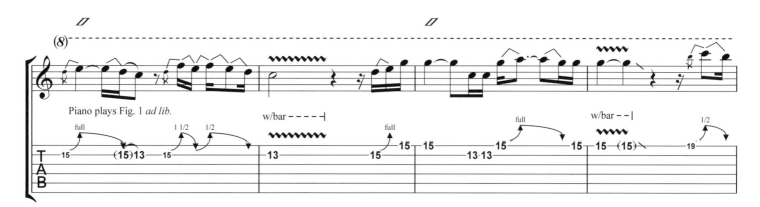

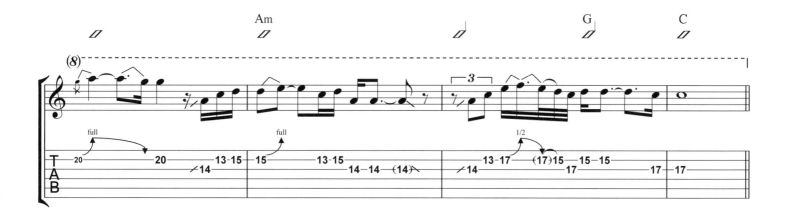

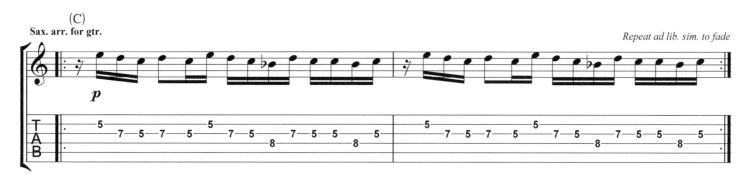

THE LOST ART OF CONVERSATION

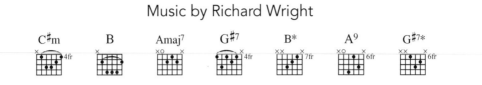

Music by Richard Wright

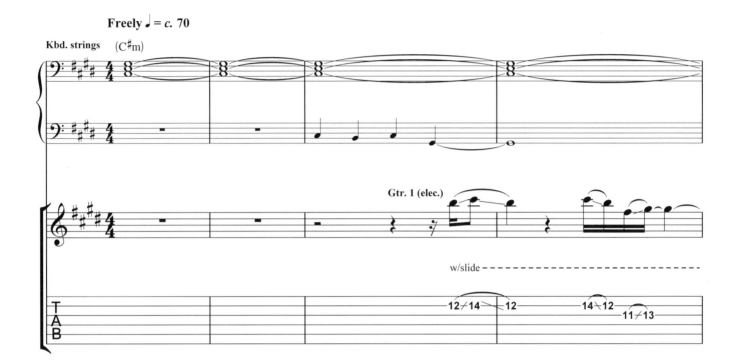

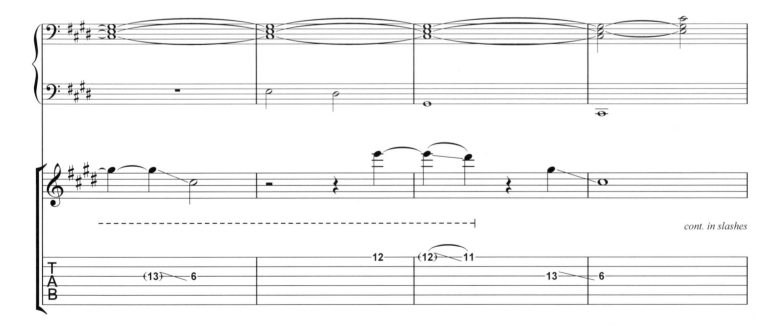

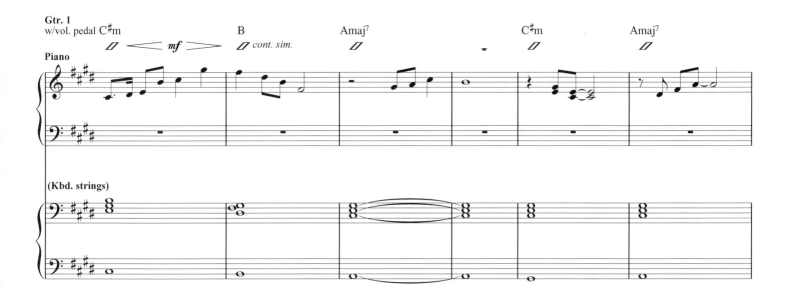

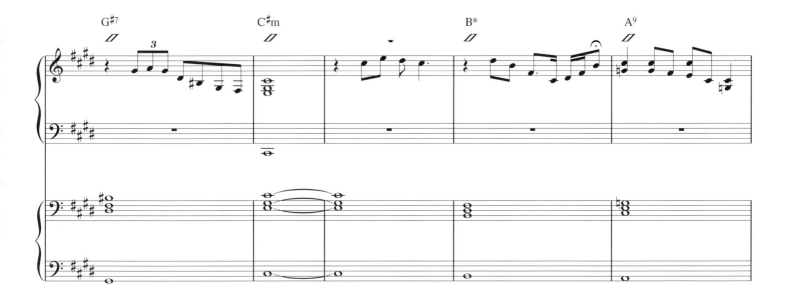

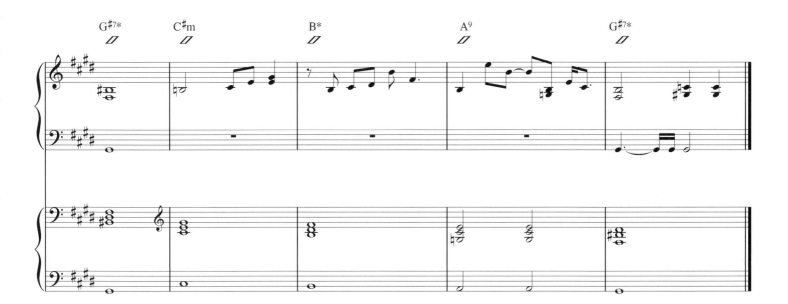

ON NOODLE STREET

Music by David Gilmour & Richard Wright

*composite part
**chords reflect overall harmony

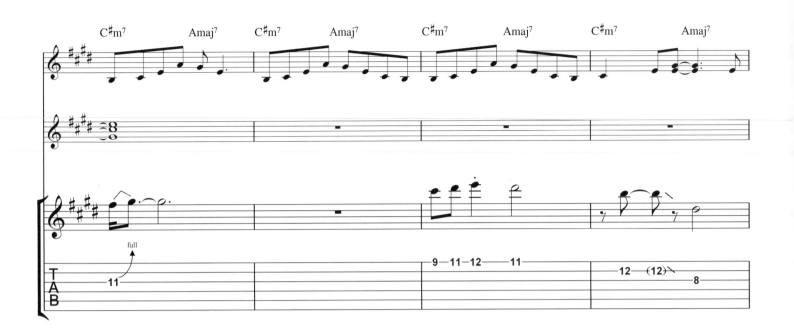

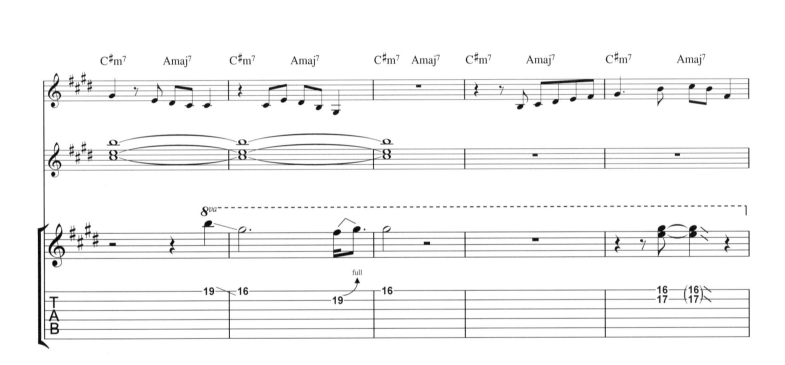

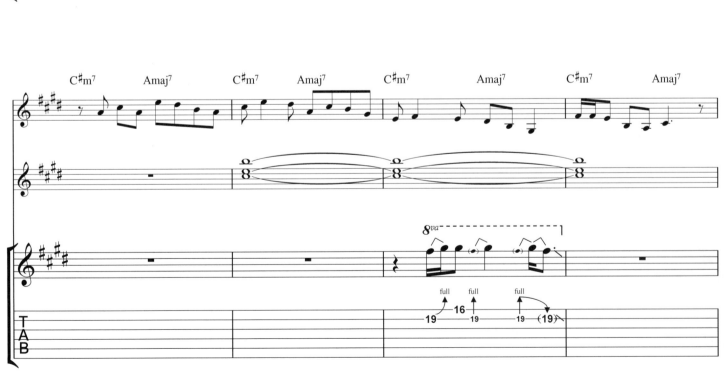

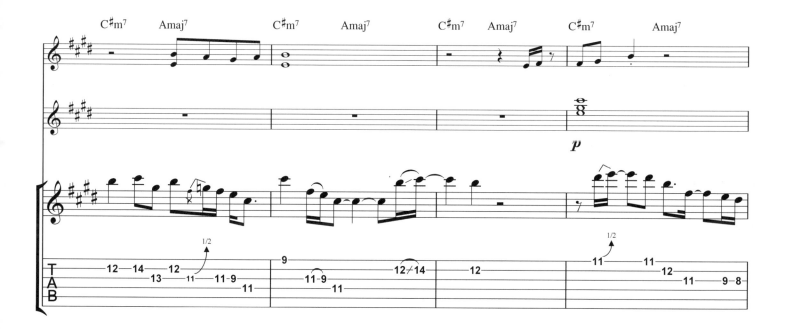

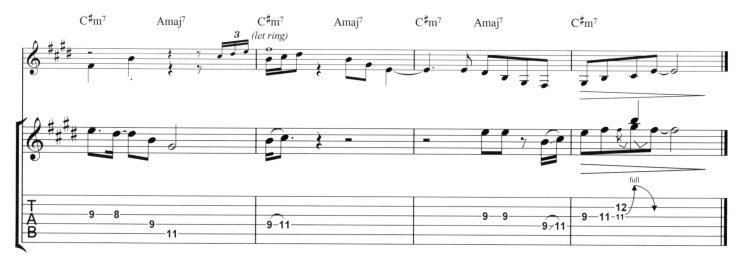

NIGHT LIGHT

Music by David Gilmour & Richard Wright

*Chords imply harmony throughout

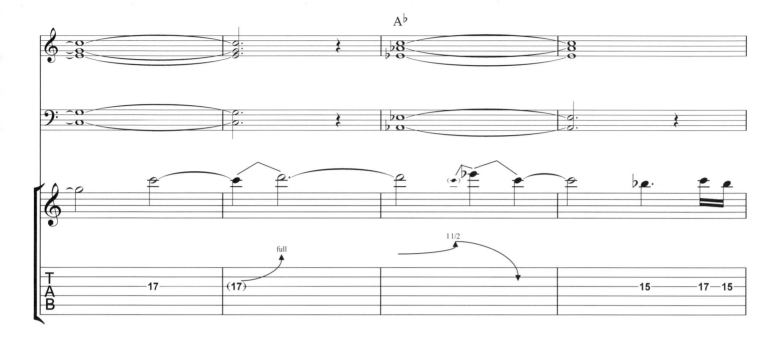

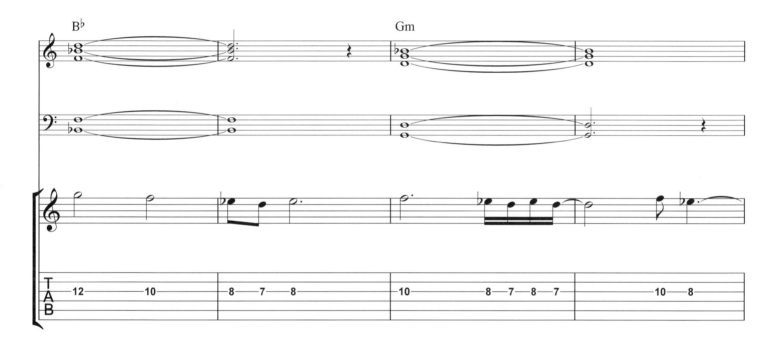

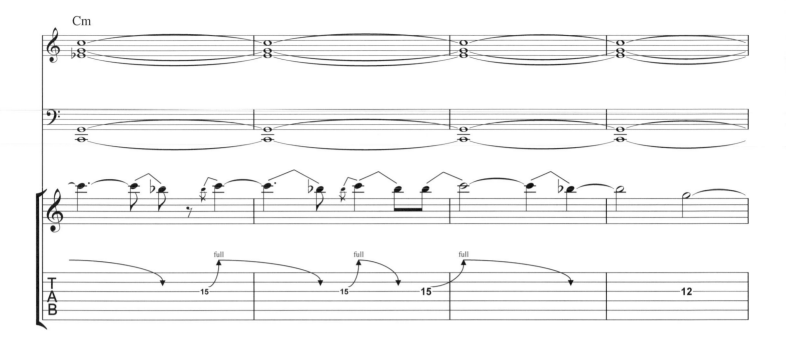

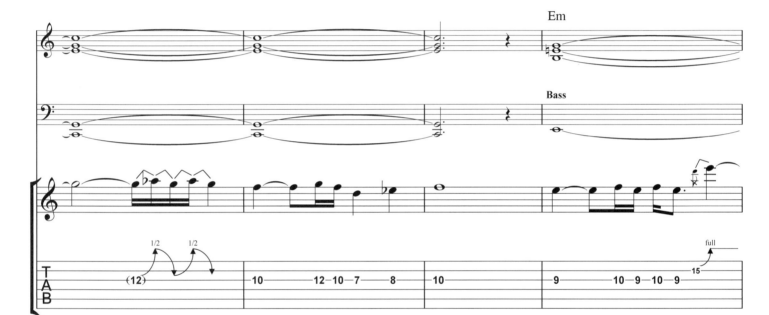

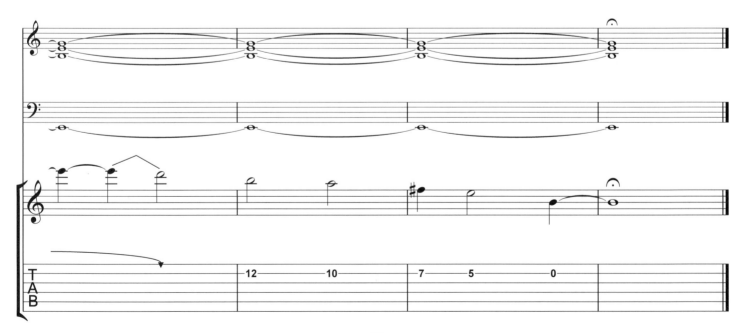

ALLONS-Y (1)

Music by David Gilmour

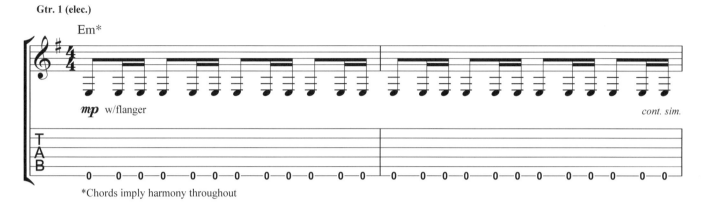

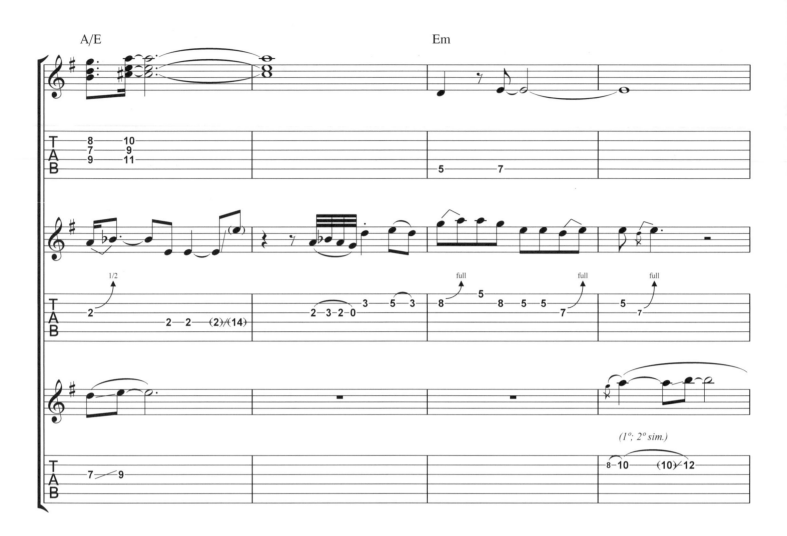

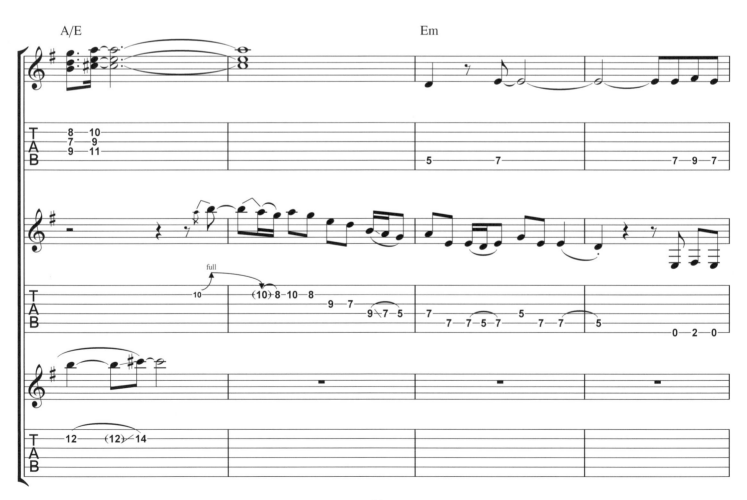

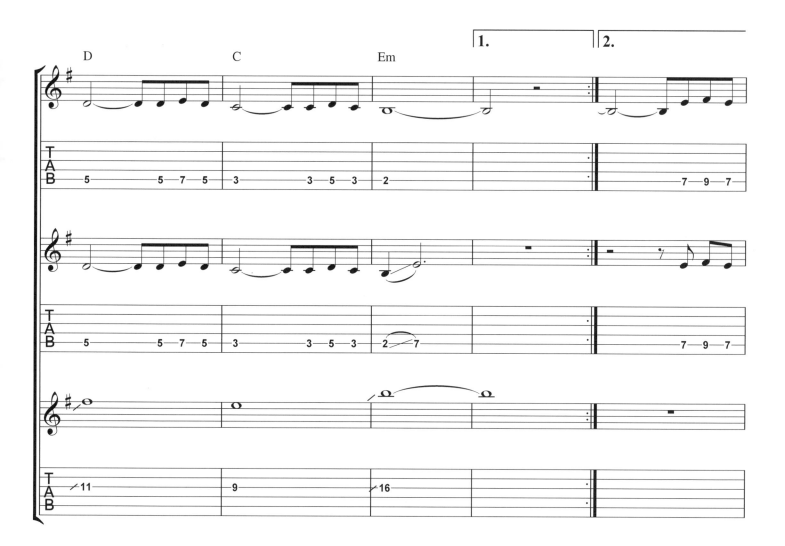

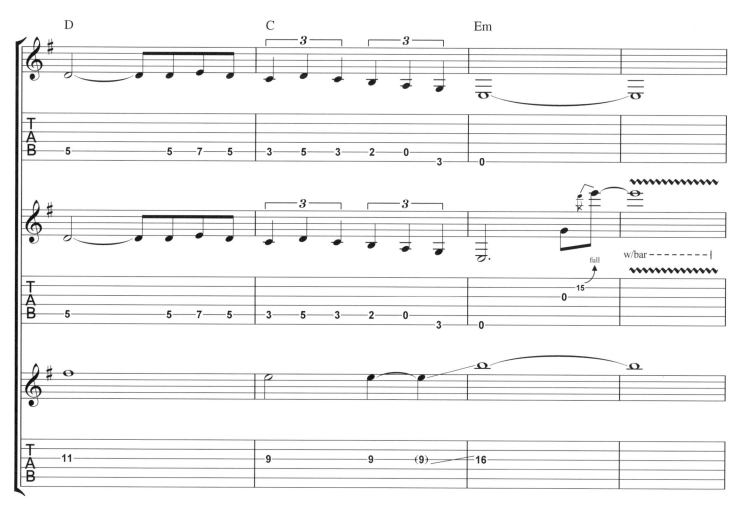

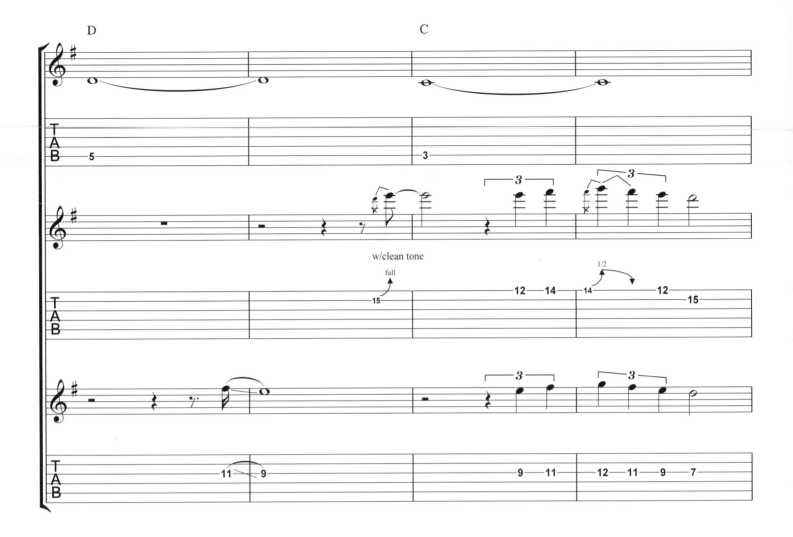

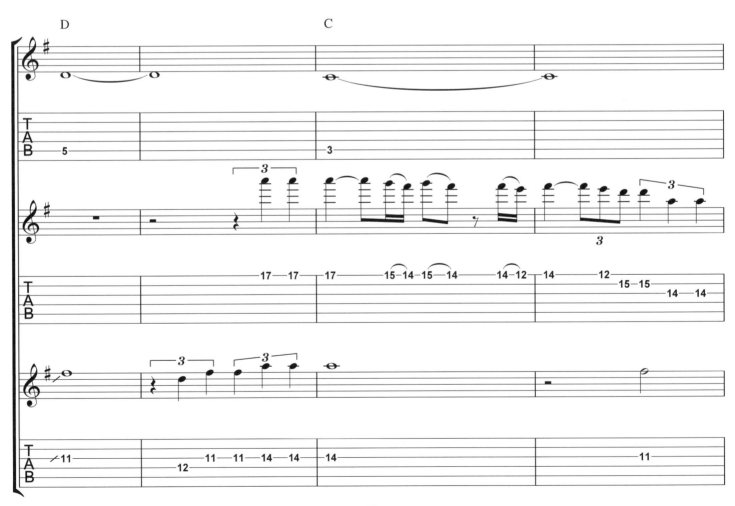

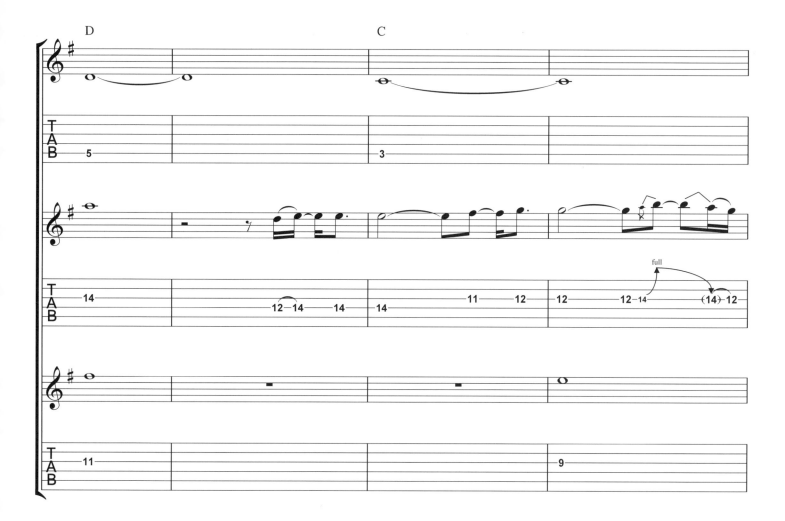

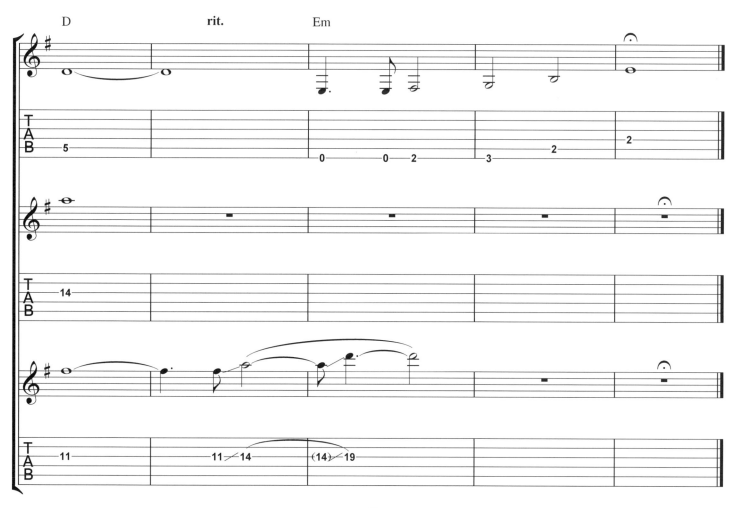

AUTUMN '68

Music by Richard Wright

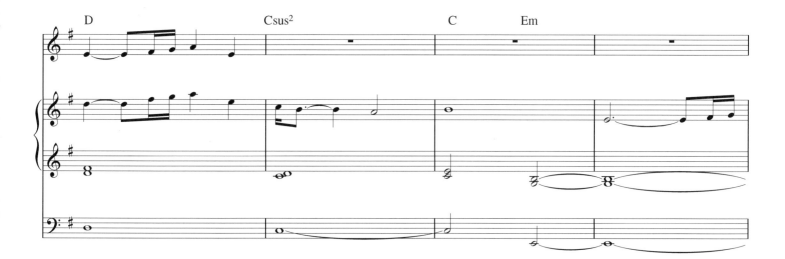

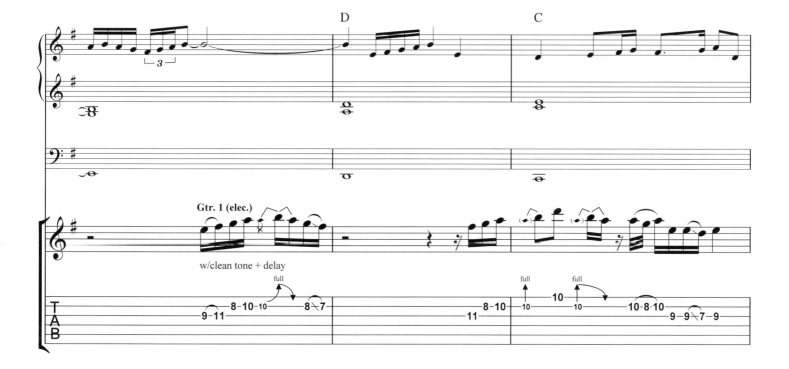

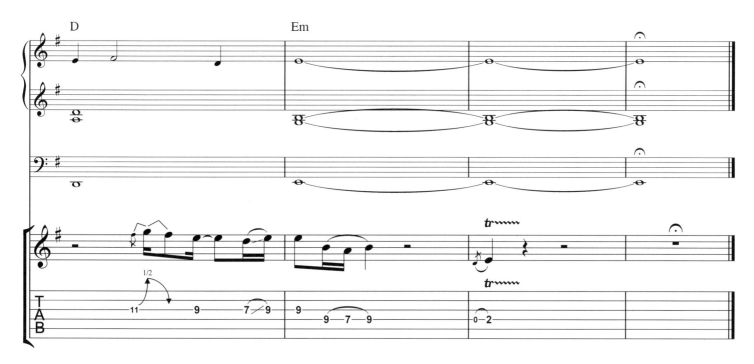

ALLONS-Y (2)

Music by David Gilmour

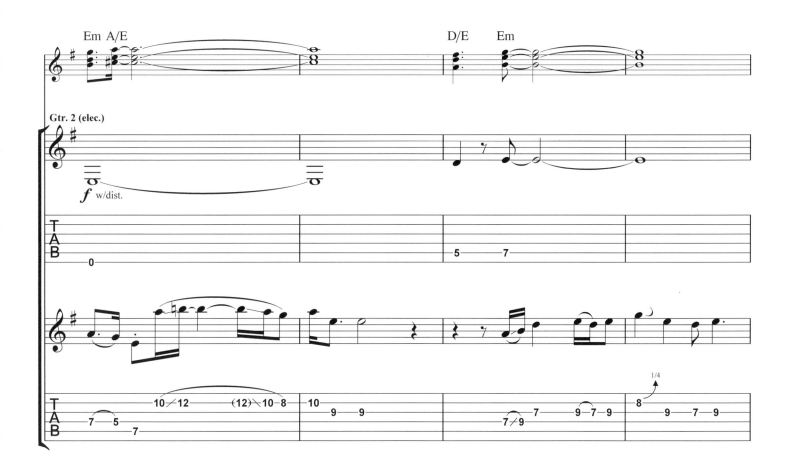

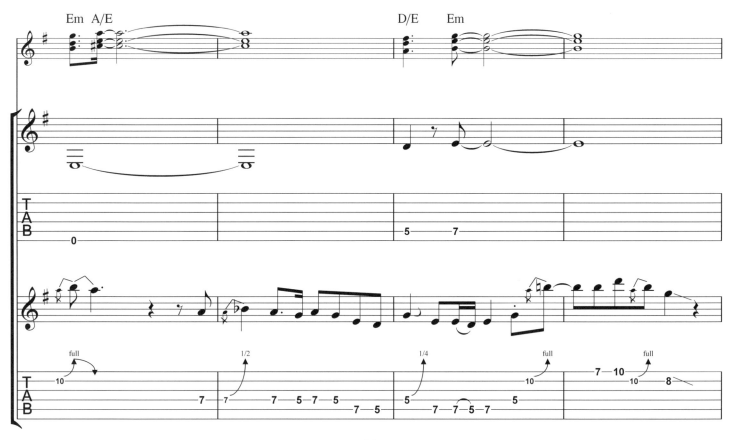

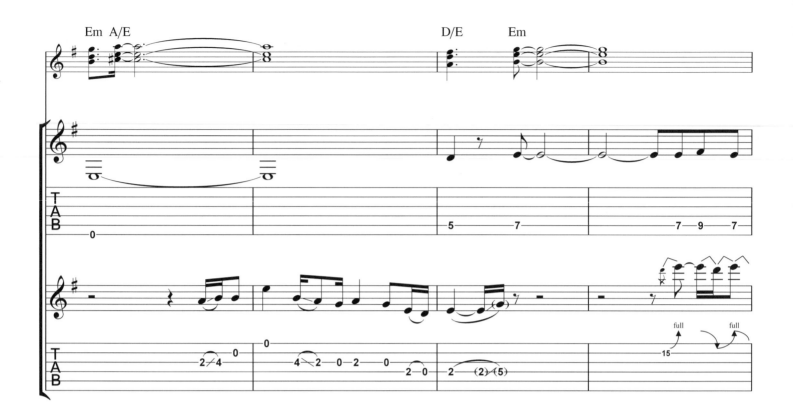

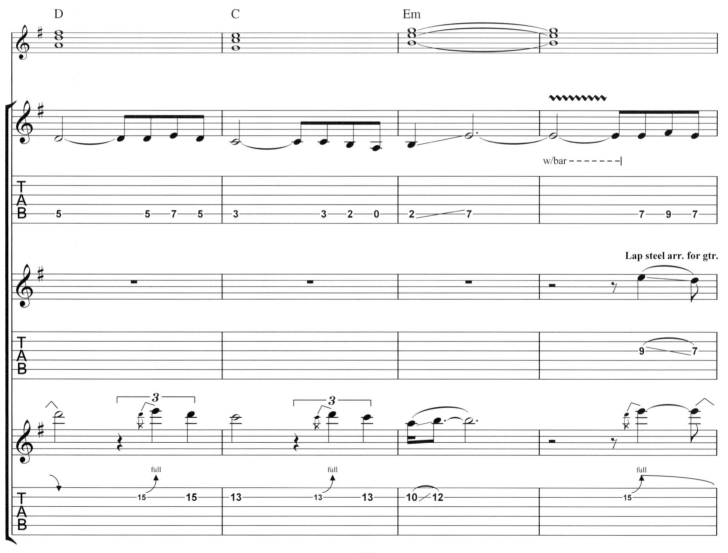

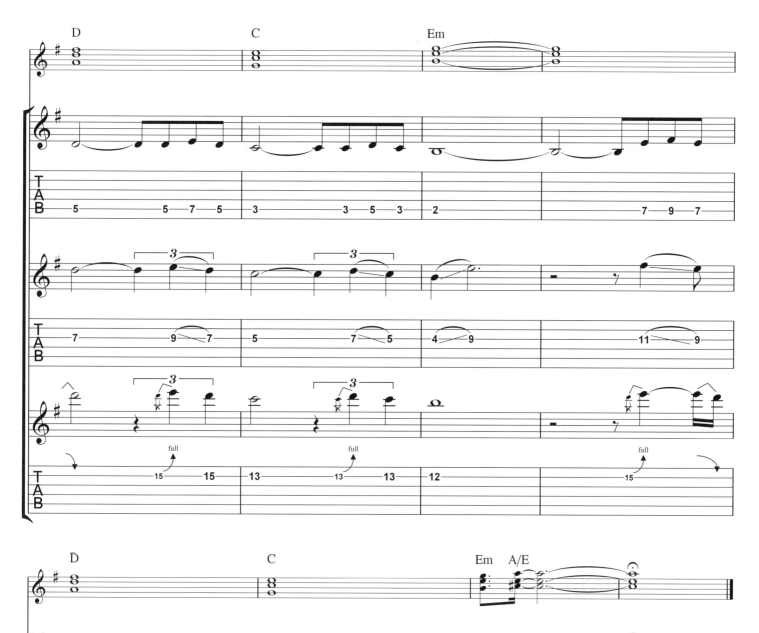

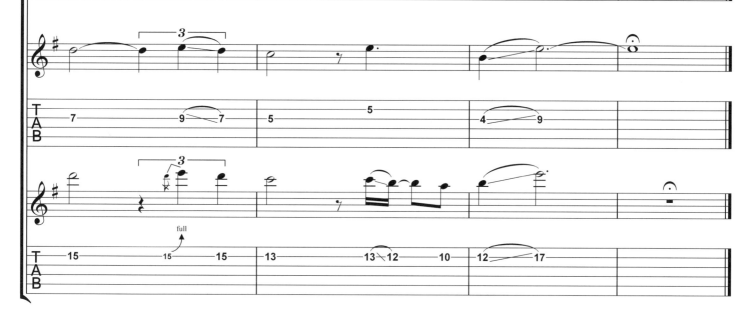

TALKIN' HAWKIN'

Music by David Gilmour & Richard Wright

*Chord names reflect piano harmony

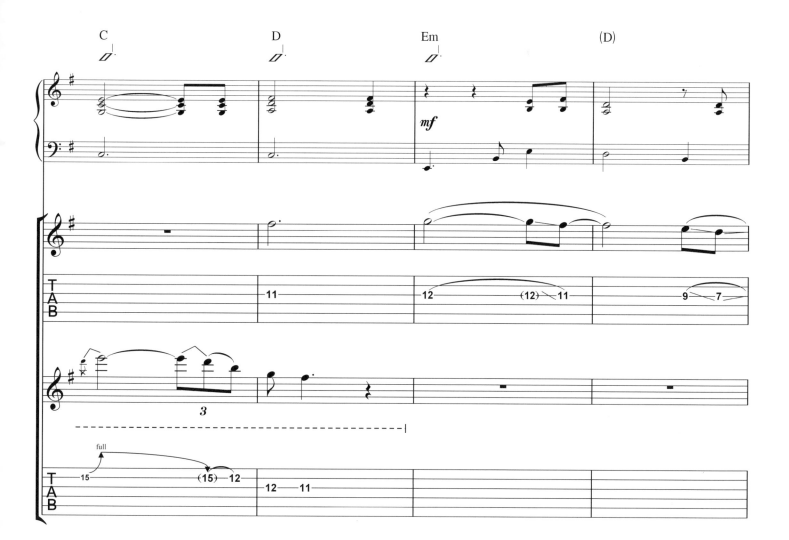

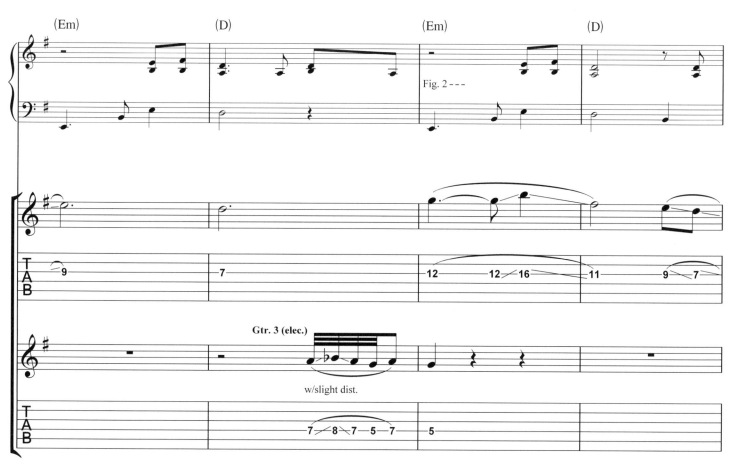

Gtr. 1 plays Fig. 1

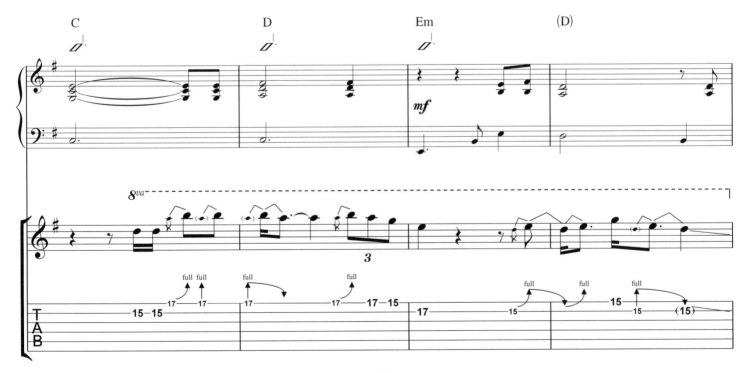

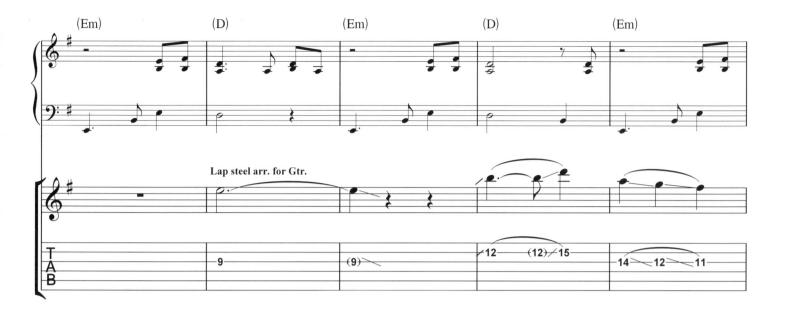

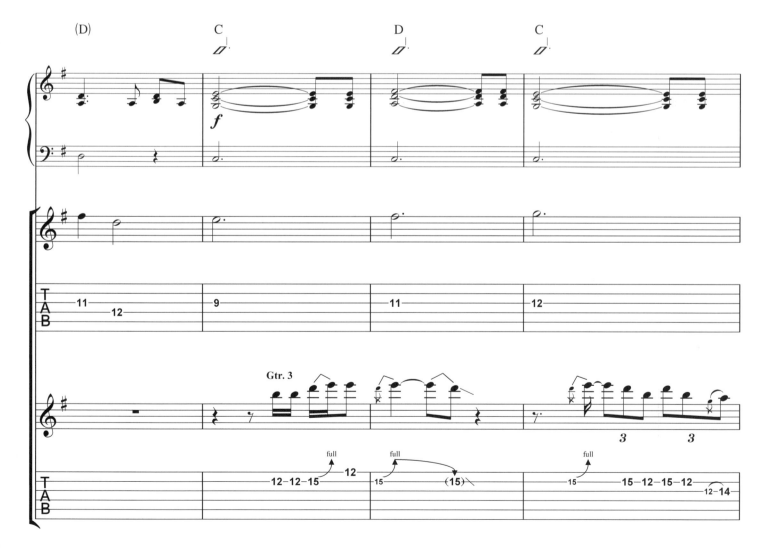

58

Our greatest

hopes could become reality in the future,   *with the technology at our disposal*   *the possibilities are unbounded.*

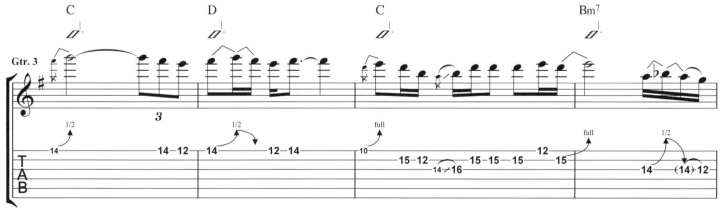

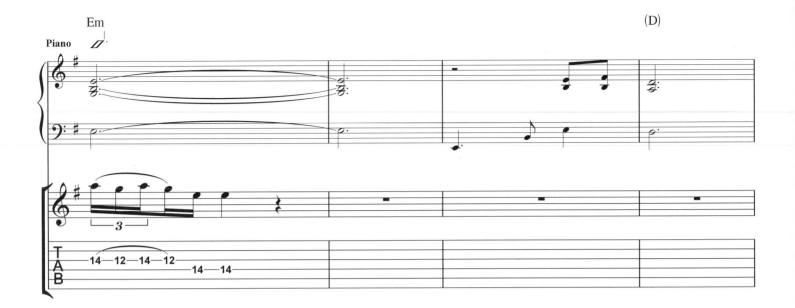

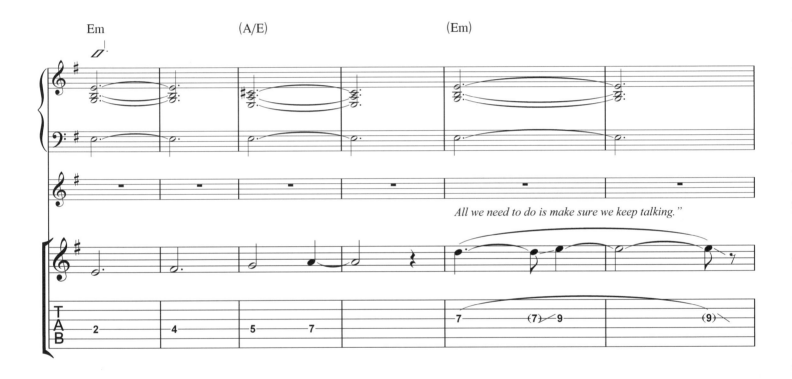

All we need to do is make sure we keep talking."

CALLING

Music by David Gilmour & Anthony Moore

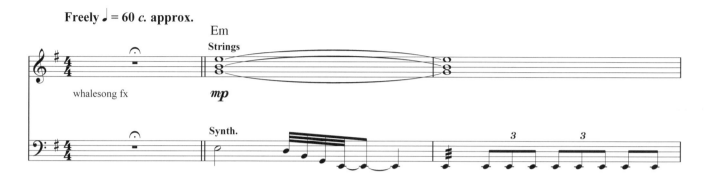

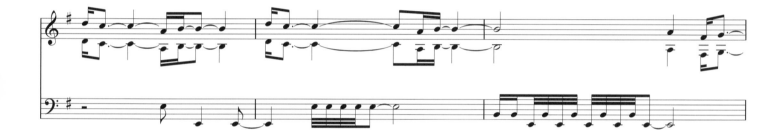

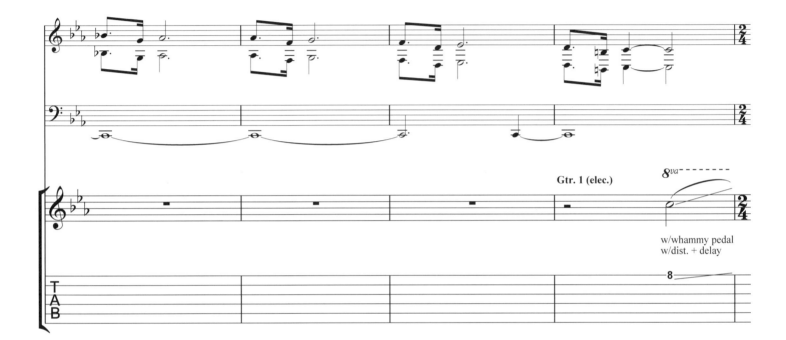

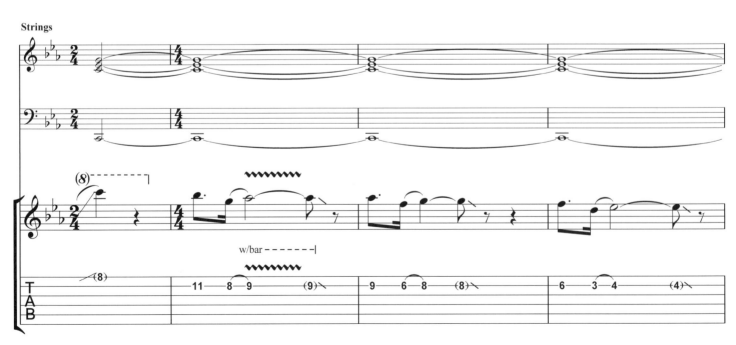

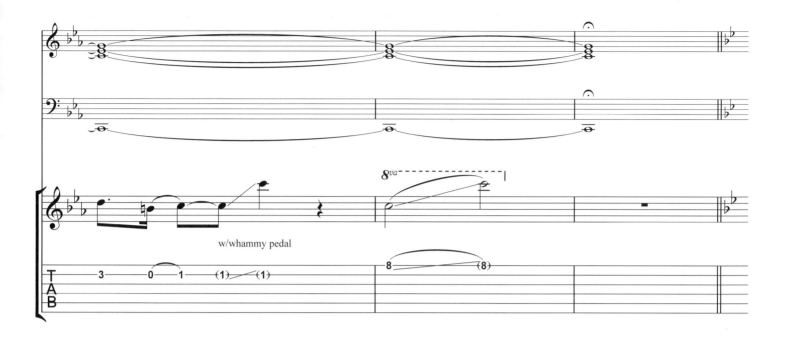

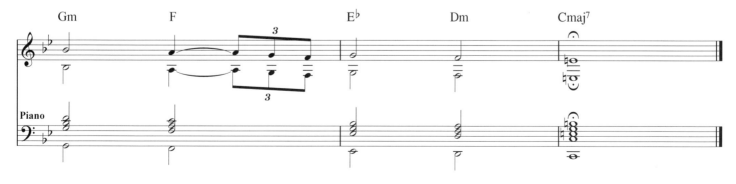

EYES TO PEARLS

Music by David Gilmour

Em

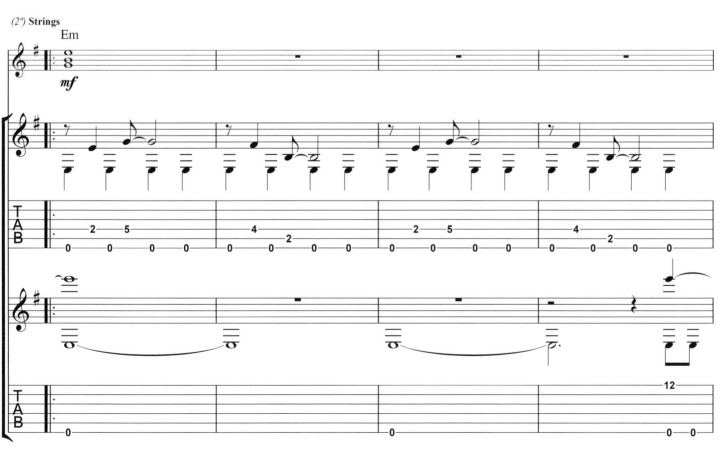

(2º) **Strings**

Em

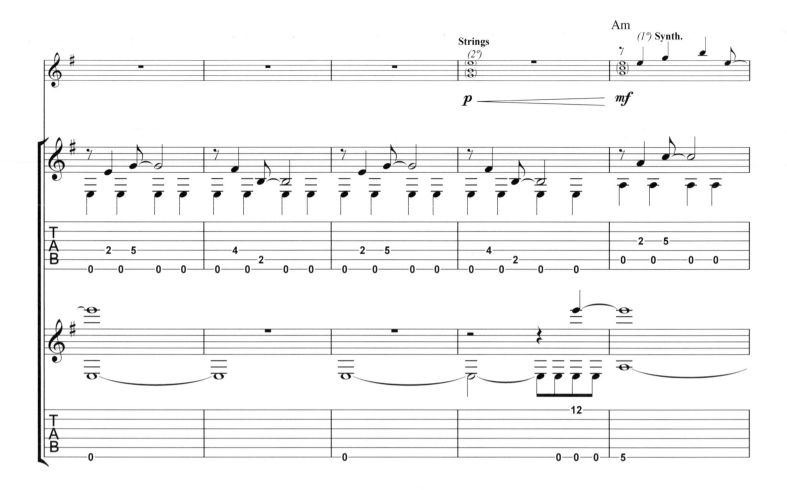

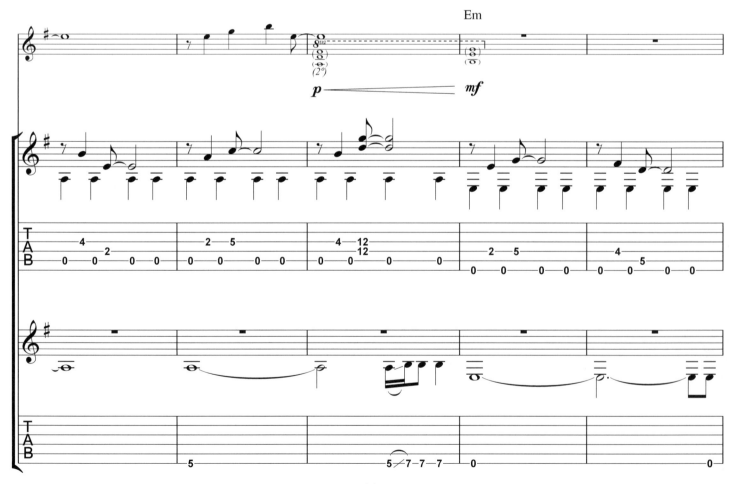

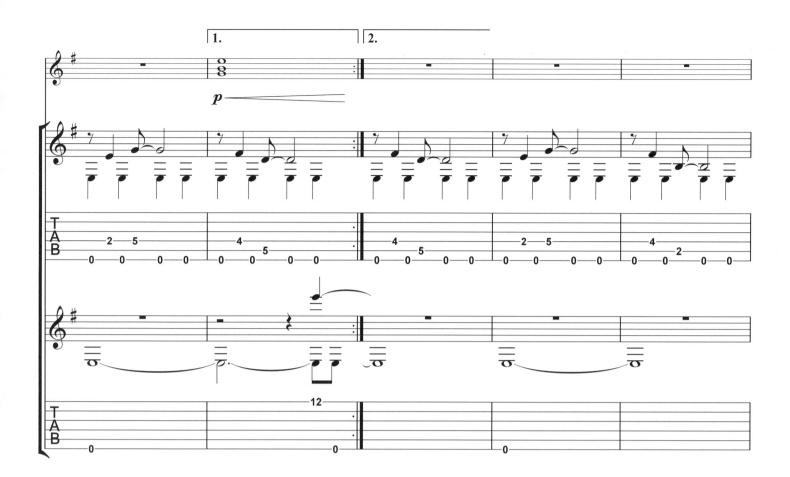

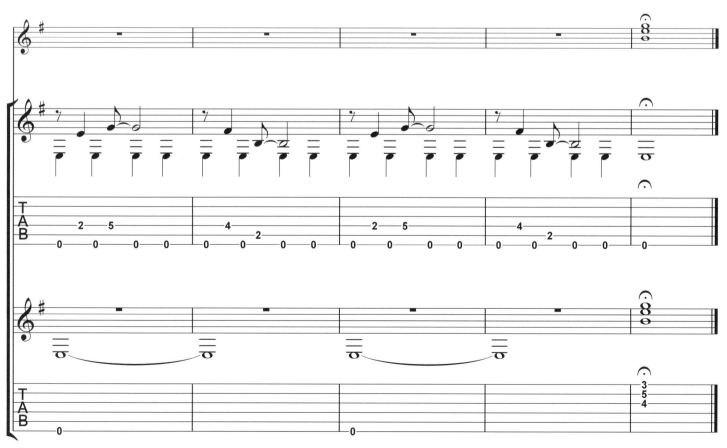

SURFACING

Music by David Gilmour

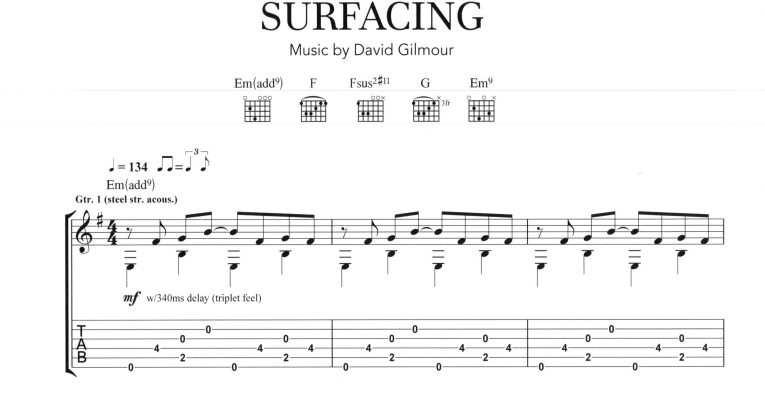

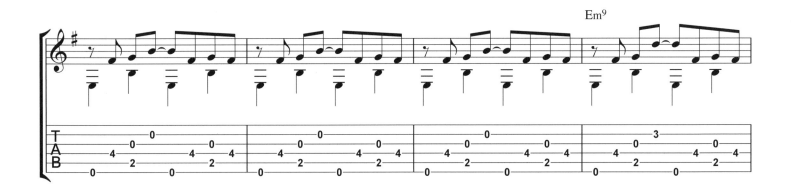

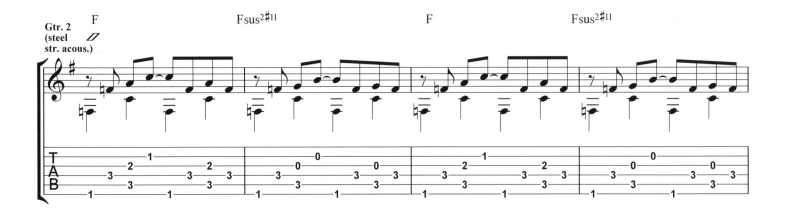

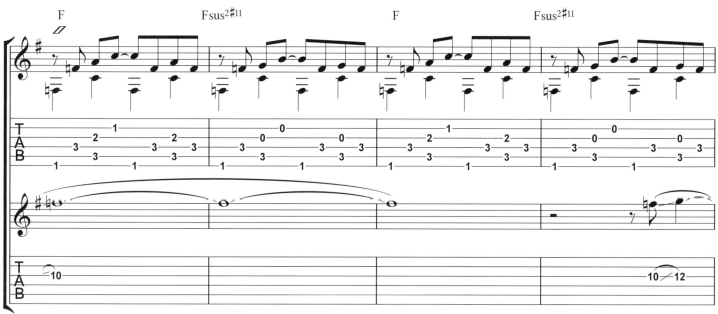

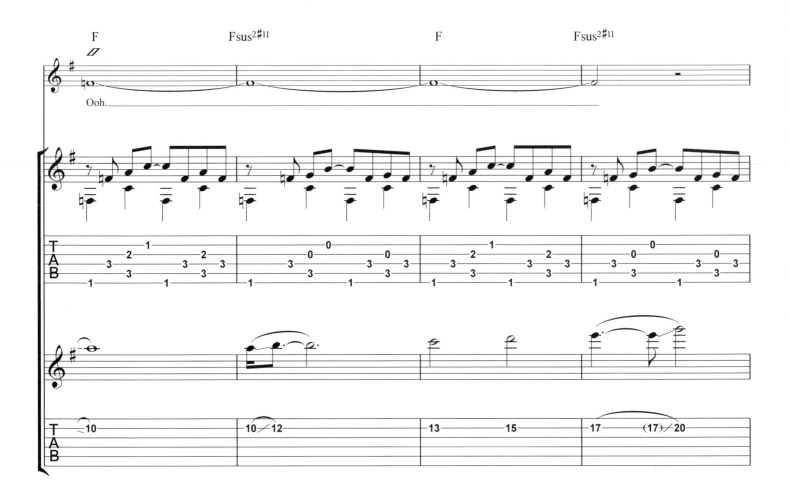

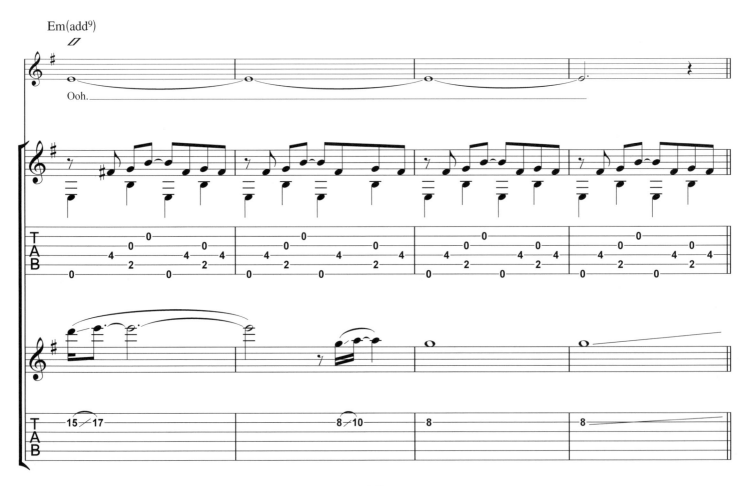

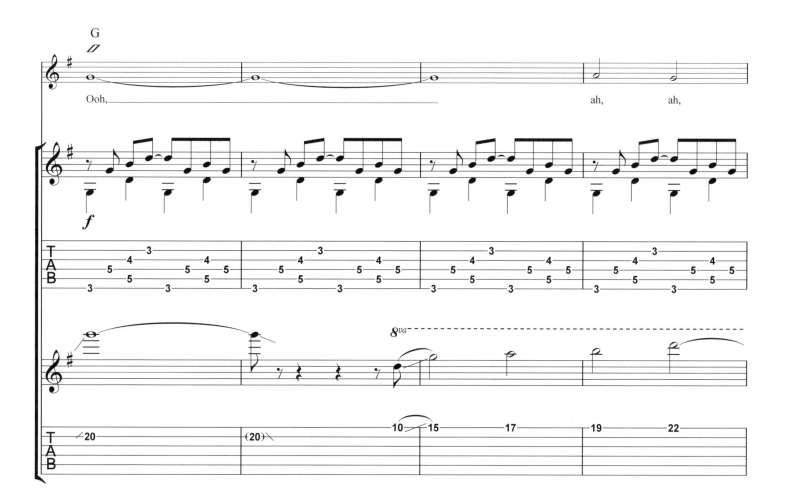

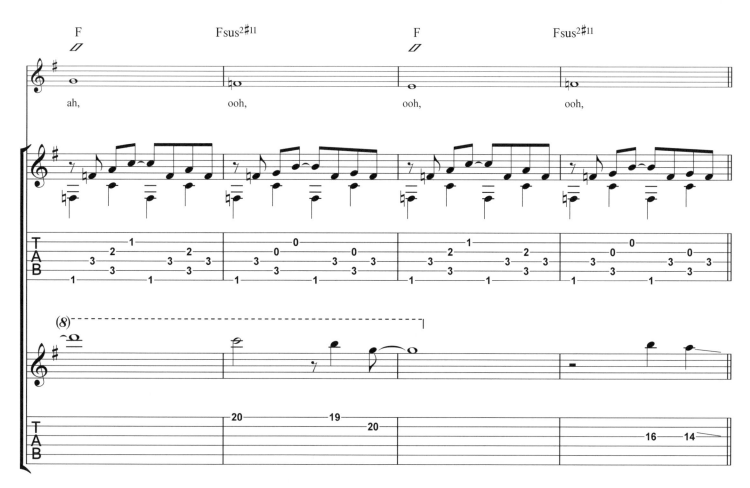

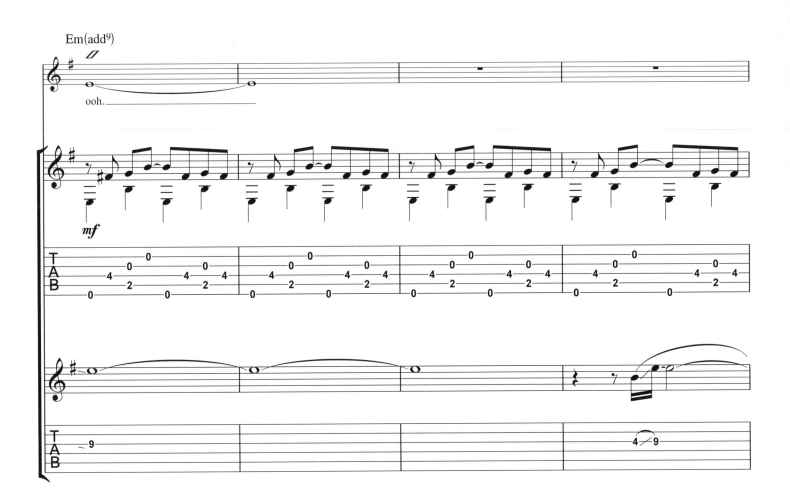

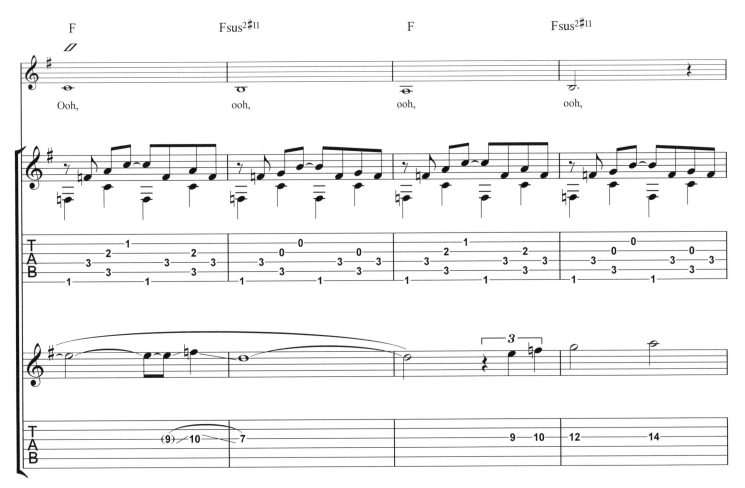

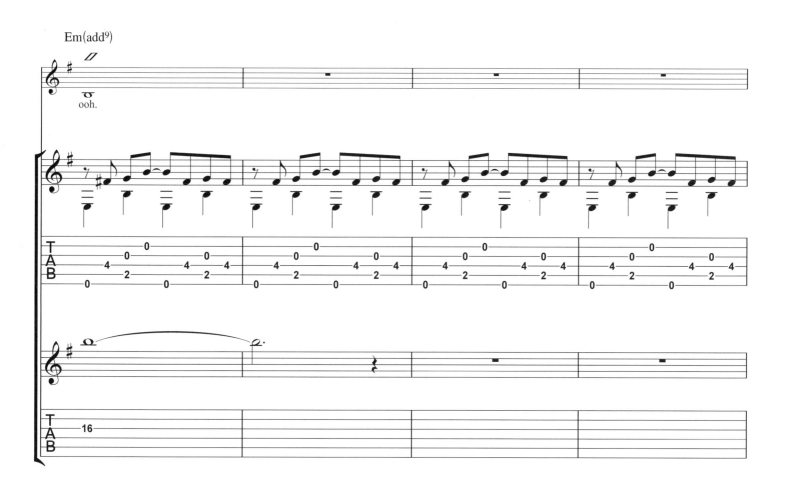

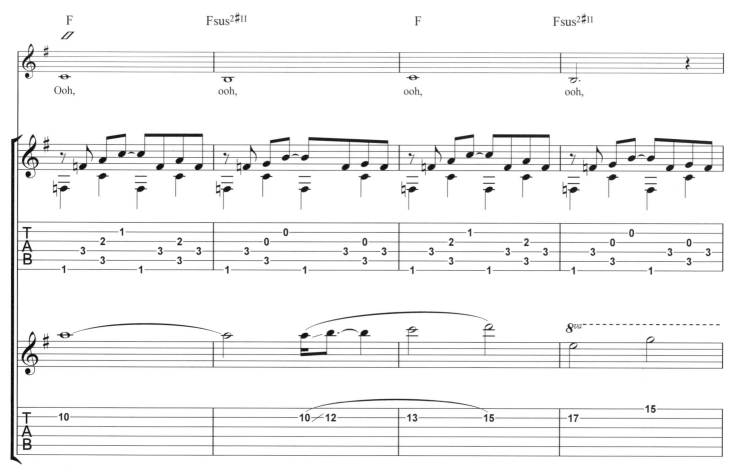

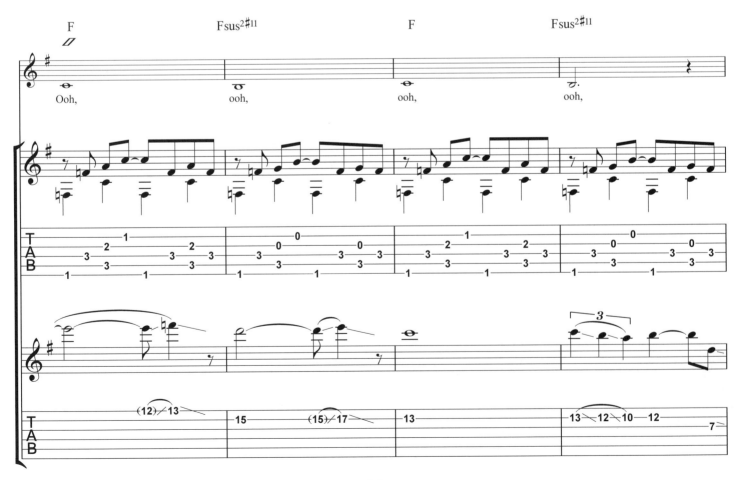

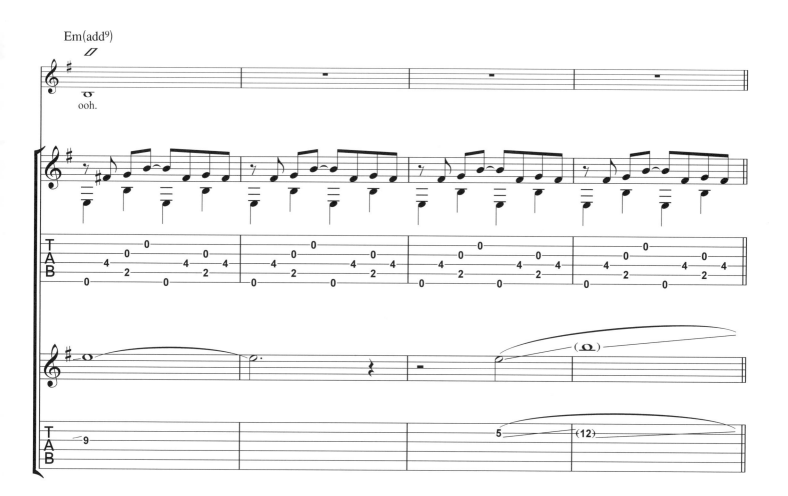

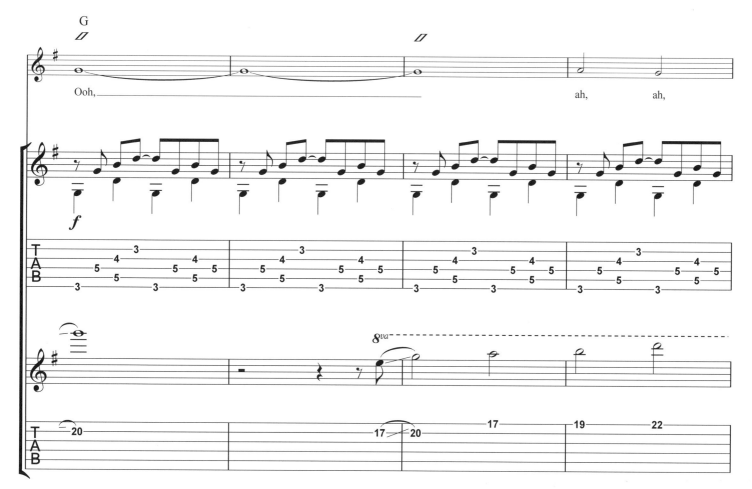

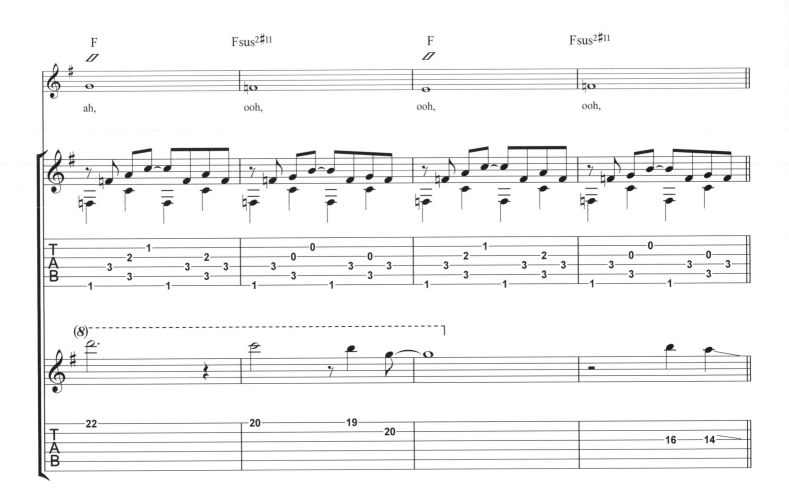

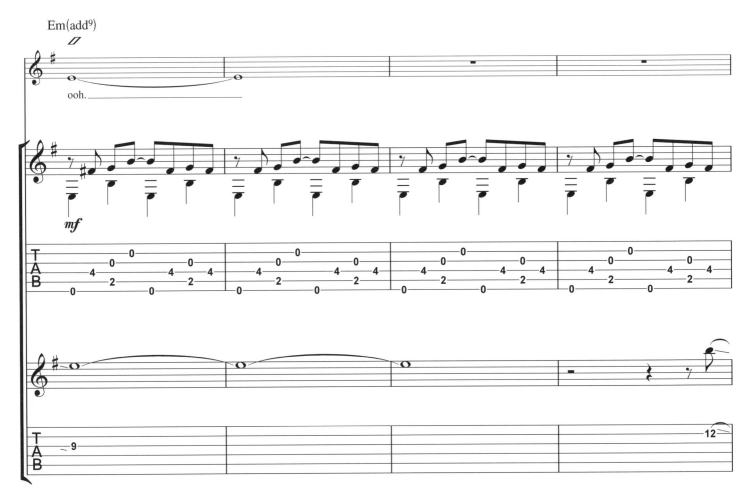

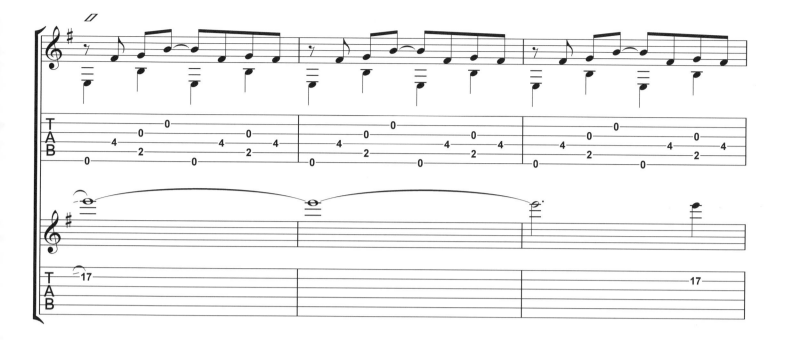

LOUDER THAN WORDS

Music by David Gilmour / Lyrics by Polly Samson

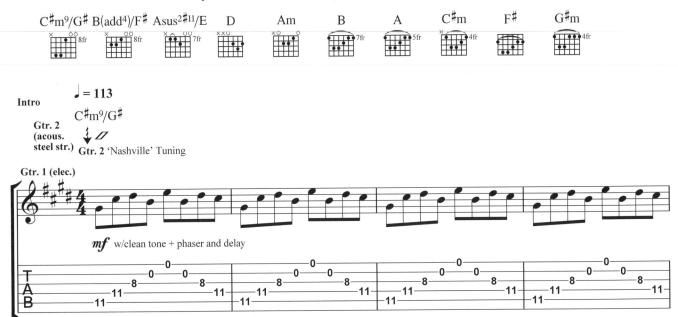

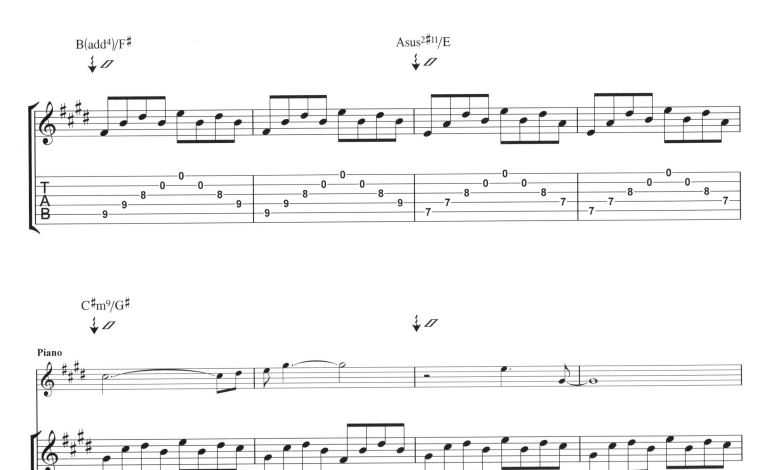

Gtrs. 2+3 are tuned to 'Nashville' tuning: the lowest four strings are replaced with the octave strings from a 12-string set, so they sound an octave higher than normal.

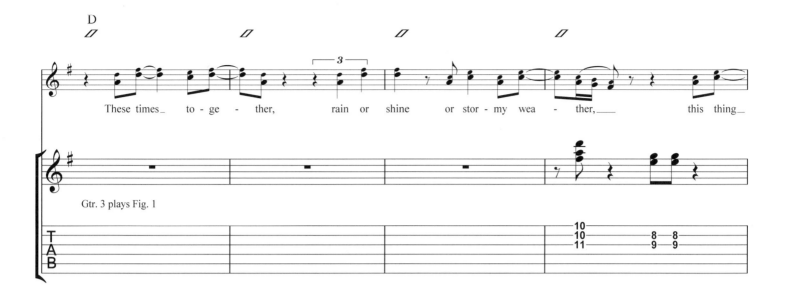

Gtr. 3 plays Fig. 1

These times_ to - ge - ther, rain or shine or stor - my wea - ther,___ this thing_

__ we_ do.__

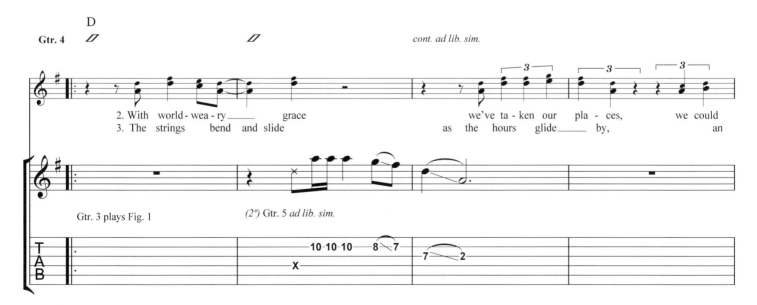

Gtr. 3 plays Fig. 1

(2°) Gtr. 5 *ad lib. sim.*

2. With world - wea - ry___ grace we've ta - ken our pla - ces, we could
3. The strings bend and slide as the hours glide___ by, an

Gtr. 3 plays Fig. 1

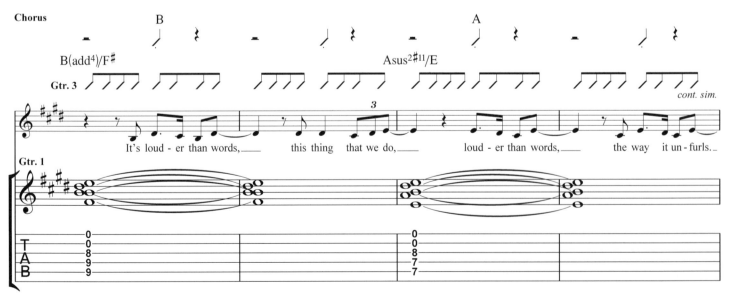

Lyrics: It's loud-er than words,___ the sum of our__ parts,___ the beat of our hearts___ is loud-er than words.___

this thing they call soul is there with a pulse,__ loud - er than words.__

Loud - er than words.__

Gtr. 1

Am

D

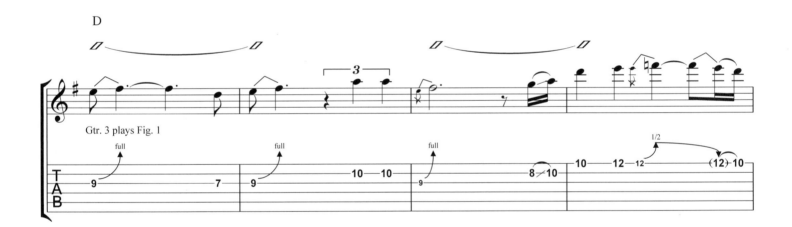

Am

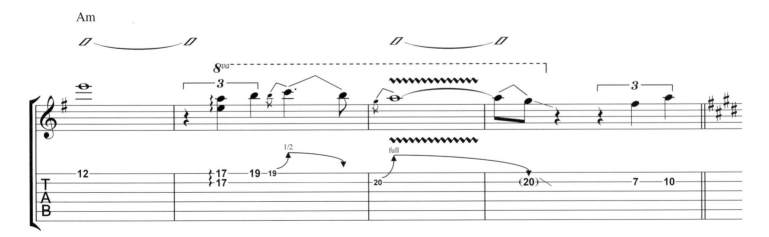

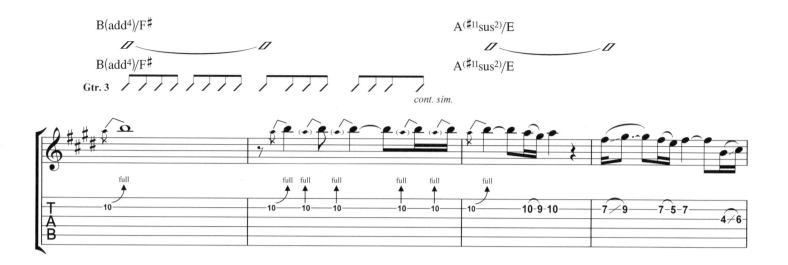

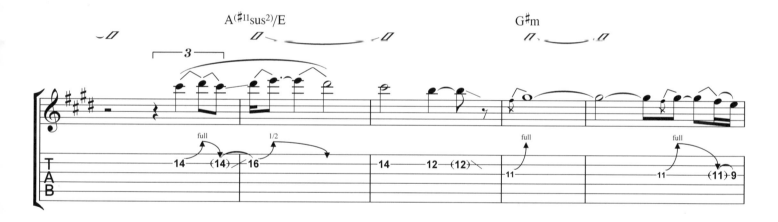

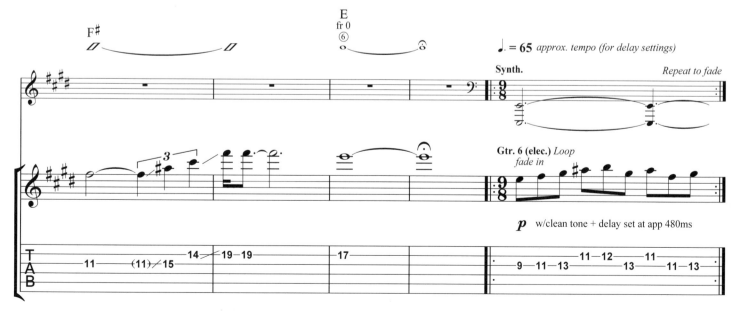

1 2 3 4 5 6 7 8 9

GUITAR TABLATURE EXPLAINED

Guitar music can be explained in three different ways: on a musical stave, in tablature, and in rhythm slashes.

RHYTHM SLASHES: are written above the stave. Strum chords in the rhythm indicated. Round noteheads indicate single notes.

THE MUSICAL STAVE: shows pitches and rhythms and is divided by lines into bars. Pitches are named after the first seven letters of the alphabet.

TABLATURE: graphically represents the guitar fingerboard. Each horizontal line represents a string, and each number represents a fret.

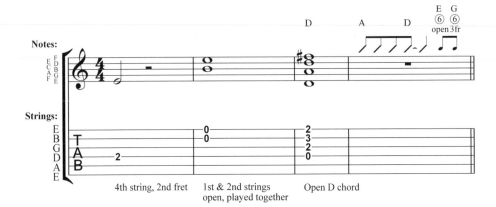

4th string, 2nd fret   1st & 2nd strings open, played together   Open D chord

Definitions for special guitar notation

SEMI-TONE BEND: Strike the note and bend up a semi-tone (½ step).

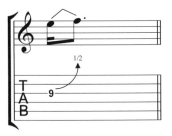

WHOLE-TONE BEND: Strike the note and bend up a whole-tone (full step).

GRACE NOTE BEND: Strike the note and bend as indicated. Play the first note as quickly as possible.

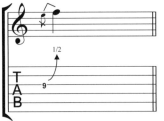

QUARTER-TONE BEND: Strike the note and bend up a ¼ step

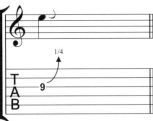

BEND & RELEASE: Strike the note and bend up as indicated, then release back to the original note.

COMPOUND BEND & RELEASE: Strike the note and bend up and down in the rhythm indicated.

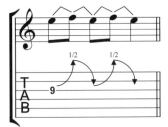

PRE-BEND: Bend the note as indicated, then strike it.

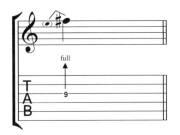

PRE-BEND & RELEASE: Bend the note as indicated. Strike it and release the note back to the original pitch.

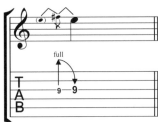

HAMMER-ON: Strike the first note with one finger, then sound the second note (on the same string) with another finger by fretting it without picking.

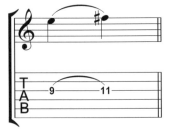

PULL-OFF: Place both fingers on the note to be sounded, strike the first note and without picking, pull the finger off to sound the second note.

LEGATO SLIDE (GLISS): Strike the first note and then slide the same fret-hand finger up or down to the second note. The second note is not struck.

MUFFLED STRINGS: A percussive sound is produced by laying the first hand across the string(s) without depressing, and striking them with the pick hand.

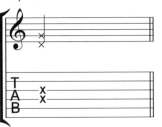

TRILL: Very rapidly alternate between the notes indicated by continuously hammering-on and pulling-off.

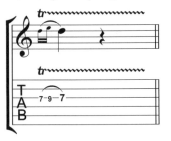

TREMOLO PICKING: The note is picked as rapidly and continously as possible.

ARPEGGIATE: Play the notes of the chord indicated by quickly rolling them from bottom to top.

SHIFT SLIDE (GLISS & RESTRIKE) Same as legato slide, except the second note is struck.